Helping in the Hallways

Practical Skills for Counselors
Jeffrey A. Kottler, Series Editor

Richard J. Hazler

Helping in the Hallways

Advanced Strategies for Enhancing School Relationships

CORWIN PRESS, INC.
A Sage Publications Company
Thousand Oaks, California

For information:

Corwin Press, Inc.
A Sage Publications Company
2455 Teller Road
Thousand Oaks, California 91320
E-mail: order@corwin.sagepub.com

SAGE Publications Ltd.
6 Bonhill Street
London EC2A 4PU
United Kingdom

SAGE Publications India Pvt. Ltd.
M-32 Market
Greater Kailash I
New Delhi 110 048 India

Printed in the United States of America

Library of Congress Cataloging-in-Publication Data

Hazler, Richard J.
  Helping in the hallways: advanced strategies for enhancing school
relationships / by Richard J. Hazler.
    p. cm.—(Practical skills for counselors)
  Includes bibliographical references.
  ISBN 0-8039-6599-0 (cloth: acid-free paper).—ISBN
0-8039-6600-8 (pbk.: acid-free paper)
    1. Educational counseling—United States. 2. Student counselors—
United States. 3. Interpersonal relations—United States.
4. School discipline—United States. 5. Schools—United States—
Safety measures. I. Title. II. Series.
  LB1027.5.H385 1997
  371.7'8—dc21   97-33762

This book is printed on acid-free paper.

98 99 00 01 02 03 10 9 8 7 6 5 4 3 2 1

Production Editor: Sherrise M. Purdum
Production Assistant: Denise Santoyo
Editorial Assistant: Kristen L. Gibson
Typesetter: Rebecca Evans
Cover Designer: Marcia M. Rosenburg

Contents

Preface

I was in my second year as the only school counselor for two small
school districts in Idaho. The first year had been a good one, and
people were happy with my work. Being the first school counselor
either district had ever hired made everything new and challenging
for me, and people were grateful for everything I did. But even with
the success, I felt frustrated. I was making a difference with some
students, but most seemed out of reach. Plenty of credit was coming
my way for scheduling, records management, letters of reference,
standardized testing, and other organizational activities, but that
hardly made a dent in the problems of students and the school that
really needed the most attention.

The students I saw were either those who were most conniving at
getting out of class or the worst problems, the ones whom teachers
wanted out of class. I felt isolated in my office, controlled by my
environment, depressed, and I was thinking about looking for another job. There was just too much to do and no way I could see to
make the impact I wanted.

One day in the midst of what was becoming a regular depression,
a teacher left a note asking to see me between periods. I never got to

the teacher during my first try that day. A basketball player stopped me to say, "Great game last night, wasn't it. It meant a lot to see you out there supporting us." Then another student whom I had never talked with before asked about taking the ACT test. I patted a shy boy on the back just walking by and got a great smile for some contact we both needed. A new student waved for my attention: She wanted me to talk with her 1st-grade sister who was still frightened about coming to her new school. Casually walking closer to two boys who seemed to be threatening a smaller boy drew their attention away from the brewing problem, and they moved on as I gave them a smile. I knew I'd never get to the teacher when a student council representative stopped me to ask if I could help with a problem the students were having with the principal. This one 5-minute break between periods gave me more productive contact with more students than I had experienced the rest of the morning.

All my best tools and training were put to use in these brief interactions. I listened, observed, gained understanding, provided support, modeled positive behaviors, offered quality advice when asked, and actually got invited into problems and issues that seemed critical to both individuals and the whole school. Even more important that particular day was the positive feedback I received about myself and my work. It was more than I had felt in a month! There was clearly something here that I had been missing, and I wanted more of it on a daily basis.

This was not my first experience with being productive in the hallways of schools, playgrounds, and businesses; but never had I personally needed it more or recognized it so clearly. Perhaps that is why this one situation sticks with me and why the concepts of hallway helping have become so important to me. The counseling office is a wonderful place where great individual progress can be made. I love that work, but I have come to realize that it has its limitations because it is also work in isolation. Having a larger influence on the school and community demands multiple brief, challenging, and supportive contacts in hallways, streets, athletic sites, playgrounds, lunchrooms, community events, coffee shops, teacher's rooms, and all the other places where people live their everyday lives. These are the places that put us in closer touch with the realities of students, faculty, administrators, parents, and even ourselves.

Finding Your Way in the Hallways

Hallways, playgrounds, and hangouts hold a wealth of joys and risks that cannot be naturally separated. They are not places to go without some idea of what you are getting into, the impact it can have on you, and how to act once you are there. Chapter 1 identifies the problems and success stories associated with schools and our society that play themselves out in the hallways. The real pressures these circumstances create and the ways people choose to face them boldly or avoid them for protection highlight the conflicting feelings you may experience.

Chapter 2 maps a path through the difficulties, advantages, and consequences of hallway involvement. Attending to key issues that we often forget in the press of the hallways will keep you prepared for productive hallway helping. The steps to turn that preparation into effective interventions are identified in Chapter 3.

The final two chapters emphasize the characteristics of specific groups and techniques that work best with each one within the hallway helping model. Chapter 4 gives attention to students who are the eventual focus of all our efforts. Essential factors that motivate adults when they come in contact with the school and specific strategies for working with them to produce a better learning climate for everyone are discussed in Chapter 5.

The model and techniques provided can be used as little or as much as you find valuable in your personal helping model. Some of you will turn directly to chapters that meet pressing needs, whereas others will read in a step-by-step pattern. If there is a right way to use the book, it is to read and make use of the information in whatever ways fit you best.

Acknowledgments

A special thanks goes to Greg Janson who was involved in this project from beginning to end. Greg thought with me, searched for ideas, and was willing and able to criticize my writing. The discussions we had on the diverse experiences of ourselves and others solidified what were sometimes vague ideas and recollections for me. We both grew in the process, which is how it should be.

Two superintendents in rural Idaho joined forces to hire one person to create new school counseling programs for both districts. Why they took a chance on an east coast outsider after only telephone interviews has never been fully answered. But Florin Hulse and Percy Christensen did exactly that and allowed me to learn firsthand about getting the most value out of a school counseling position. We learned together about helping in the hallways, and for that I am forever grateful.

Those who kept me on track throughout the writing of this book were friends such as Judy Morgan, a longtime school counselor; series editor Jeffrey Kottler; and many others who helped in the ways they could when I needed it.

My wife Kitty has been there through all the changing, the frustrations, the joy, the experiencing, and the writing. Many thanks go to her and to our two daughters, Shannon and Erin, who make us so proud.

Richard J. Hazler

About the Author

Richard J. Hazler is Professor of Counselor Education at Ohio University in Athens, Ohio, where he lives with his wife, Kitty. He has two grown daughters, Shannon and Erin. He did graduate work at Trenton State College, New Jersey, and earned his PhD at the University of Idaho. He has been a school counselor and has also counseled in the military, universities, a prison, and private practice. In addition, he has been an elementary school teacher, writer, and director of a variety of programs for young people. He has authored professional materials and research on a variety of topics, including bullying and victimization in schools, and he has authored numerous articles and books. His most recent books include *Breaking the Cycle of Violence: Interventions for Bullying and Victimization* (1996) and *What You Didn't Learn in Graduate School: A Survival Guide for Therapists* (1997), with Jeffrey Kottler. He has also appeared on national television on the "Leeza Gibbons Show" and "Life Choices."

1

Hazardous Hallways

The realities of student life are not found in classrooms and school offices. It is in the hallways and on the playgrounds where kindergartners first get lost and scared only to later develop confidence as they find their way around. It is here that bigger kids try pushing others around until someone or something stops them, and smaller kids gain confidence by learning how to hold onto seats on the bus or places in line. Some children are blessed with invitations into a group, and others are shunned. Threats, punishments, praise, and plans can all be parts of quick trips to the rest room. Tears over college board exams and plans to get a car for the dance play themselves out in school parking lots and local hangouts. The illusion of a sanitized academic life that we fabricate in our classrooms and counseling offices is stripped away in the hallways. What remains is the best and worst of real life. Our training and commitment as counselors and educators is sorely needed in this hallway world, but our training has not focused on how to make the greatest impact there.

A trip through the hallways is no simple excursion for professionals. Problems, confusion, sorrows, frustrations, and anxieties are there for anyone who wants to help. Attend to them and you can make a difference. Duck out of the way and you have done much less than is possible. There are a wealth of pleasures, excitement, fun, and accomplishments waiting to be recognized and enjoyed in the hallways. Your simple presence, a smile of recognition, a pat on the back, or an offer of support can do wonders for students and also for yourself. But forget to congratulate someone on her newest source of pride or fail to recognize a meekly waved hello, and you can be seen as just another noncaring adult. Rules are less clear once you get outside school offices and classrooms, which makes the risks higher, but this also creates opportunities as well. Circumstances outside the classroom offer more freedom to act on life's realities and the chance for immediate impact that is not available in more formal environments.

What problems make hallways more hazardous today? What can schools and communities do to strengthen the best that hallways have to offer and minimize their inherent problems? How can counselors and educators at all levels make the most of these situations with the professional skills we already have and in the limited time available?

These are the questions explored in this book. Heaven knows you have more than enough to do already, and this book should not add to that burden. Instead, it provides short, quick interventions into the everyday events that take place all around you. They take little time or planning and reap new rewards for everyone, including you.

Mounting Pressures

It seems that everyone in education is being asked to do more with less even as the problems we must deal with worsen. It doesn't take much to see that schools are not the safe places they once were. Professionals today have widely different challenges to deal with than they did in 1940 when teachers rated their top disciplinary problems as talking out of turn, chewing gum, making noise, running in the hall, cutting in line, and questioning dress code violations. Fifty years later, those problems might seem like the concerns of the model school. Now we face responsibility for prevention, intervention, and remediation of situations with a much higher level of violence and dangerous consequences. In the 1990s, teachers identified problems they face as assault, robbery, drug abuse, pregnancy, and suicide (Toch, 1993).

Creating safe, disciplined, and drug-free schools was one of six key goals identified by the 1993 National Education Goals Panel. The panel's 1996 follow-up report did not bode well for reaching those goals any time in the near future. Drug use and drug sales on school grounds were up; alcohol use had stayed the same; 30% more teachers reported being threatened in school; and discipline problems were increasingly interfering with instruction. Apparently our crack government planners missed something significant:

Interpersonal improvements come from emphasizing relationships among everyone involved, not edicts, goals, and demands to change.

Academic issues make up the bulk of the National Education Goals 2000, and these did not fare well either. The millions we as a nation put into increased testing and goal setting at all levels have not changed the fact that reading achievement in grade schools stayed the same, and achievement actually decreased as students got older. School drop-out rates have remained constant. A particularly disturbing finding was that even with all the effort being put into dealing with diversity, the disparity in achievement between white students and students of color increased. Progress appears to be slow at best, no matter what the student's age, but it is even worse for females, for those who look "different," and for those who come from another culture.

The disequilibrium, anxiety, tension, and high emotional levels found in schools can create havoc among individuals and groups. The most ancient reaction to such pressures is to up the ante by promoting more rules, harsher rules, and more cumulative consequences to those who break the rules—even though this model has had little success. In fact, more stringent rules demand more active enforcement, which creates a whole new set of pressures on those with the least influence and quietest voices. They become the most likely to be ignored in favor of the loud and powerful. Antagonistic actions are often the result rather than the calming influence that increased rule making was designed to promote.

Three counselors who spend extensive time working in the hallways described their observations:

- "Sometimes it feels like we'd be better trained as drill sergeants. Keep moving, get in step, don't look sideways or you'll be put down. It is not an enjoyable way to live."
- "Strike three and you're out is big here. Who cares whether the discipline citations were for carrying guns or dozing in class. The stricter we get, the more logic goes out the window."
- "The school and its rules are a mess that hurts everyone. My job is to clean up the mess day after day like an emotional janitor."

Other counselors at a recent conference expressed strong opinions on how various groups in the school were being affected by the increasing tension levels:

- "Students have lost hope for any logic, common sense, or that their own beliefs might be part of the rules. They blame adults and see no reason to take responsibility for what goes on."
- "Parents are just plain angry and frustrated. They feel disconnected and have lost respect for school professionals."
- "Teachers feel isolated and unsupported. They will take any shoulder that offers just a little comfort and understanding."
- "Administrators are paid more money to be in charge, but even they complain of feeling helpless."

So who is benefiting from more tests, more rules, and stronger consequences? This is a good question without a solid answer for schools or society as a whole. Government is spending more on law enforcement, yet we feel less secure. We catch more people breaking an increasing number of laws, and then we put more of them behind bars for longer sentences. And still we feel less safe and have to pay more for police protection and prisons.

Research also tells us that simply making tougher rules is not the answer. Five-minute time-outs for students do as much good as 20-minute time-outs (McGuffin, 1991). The deterioration of troubled families is generally accompanied by a pattern of creating more and harsher rules that have no positive effect. In fact, just the opposite occurs, as the increasing demands seem to pump up the pressures and speed up the decline (Miller & Prinz, 1990). It is clear that additional force alone is not the way to handle our increasing problems.

Anger and frustration from developmental differences, unequal abilities, racial bias, sexual discrimination, socioeconomic prejudices, and power imbalances between groups and individuals cannot be legislated or punished away. Long-term hope for our schools lies in the relationship of building knowledge, skills, and practices that caring professionals and parents are willing to implement in real-world hallways.

Hope in the Hallways

We cannot eliminate the history of punishments and reinforcements that can cause us to relate to others in a "Whose fault is it?" model. However, a present and future model can be used to change the ways we work on school relationships. What has been found to be effective is a diligent implementation of more personal involvement by professionals in shaping real-life relationships between everyone in a community. Taking time to demonstrate positive relationships in the hallways and streets where such relationships are not normally invited will produce the beneficial changes we are seeking.

Why does Browne Junior High in the middle of troubled Washington, D.C., have a history of academic success and an attendance rate of 92%? Credit is given to a principal who knows every student by name, a staff whose words and actions show pride and belief in their students, and a school in which people are demonstrative and energetic and in which the parents know the staff because of their involvement in the community. *Outside* the offices and classrooms are where these differences are being made.

How does another Washington, D.C., junior high transform itself from an unruly school with massive discipline problems and poor attendance into a model school? Hine Junior High still has poor plumbing and bad security problems, but the atmosphere and actions of the students and staff have changed dramatically, and they now can hold their heads high. This was a result in large part of the staff's increasing involvement with the hallway and street lives of their students, in addition to attending more closely to only "a few basic rules" that are understood and accepted by almost everyone.

A Catholic elementary school for the arts exists in a crime-ridden neighborhood of the Bronx, New York, where 75% of the students come from one-parent families, 20% have one or more parents with a substance abuse problem, and 30% live on public assistance. Why is this school thriving with unity, pride, hope, and success, even after fire destroyed two thirds of their main building? One student summed up the feelings of many: "The teachers care about us. They want us to succeed, to go on in life." A mother put it another way: "It wouldn't matter if the classes were in the alley. It's the spirit of the place that counts for kids in this kind of community."

What does this small handful of hopeful stories have in common? It was not loads of money, the elimination of poverty, the eradication of prejudice, or continual development of newer and stricter rules that made the difference. The professionals in these schools are moving outside their offices and classrooms to tap the positive potential of more casual relationships within schools and communities. School counselors and other dedicated professionals are right in the middle of initiating this growth and making it work.

These schools are places where kids like to be and where the professionals are feeling better about their work than they have in years. Of course, resistance to change is a factor in even the best of circumstances. When you have figured out how to do your job with a degree of success, it is no easy step to move into uncharted waters. What overcomes the resistance and encourages and solidifies these risky steps are the benefits that come with the more personalized interactions and camaraderie. School becomes a place where you can both find support for yourself and give it as needed for day and life transitions. These are schools where a few key people begin to consistently exemplify to everyone the hallway characteristics of joy, excitement, hope, support, and adventure. Others follow later as they begin to see on a daily basis how the new approach can directly improve their lives.

These positive interpersonal relationships are directly reflected in the characteristics of safer schools that are generally smaller or encourage cohort relationships so that people can get to know each other better. Classrooms are well disciplined so that positive aspects of relationships can be more fully explored. These are the schools where students, faculty, and parents alike recognize and appreciate a connectedness between the classroom, the hallways, and the neighborhood.

Students in safer schools truly believe they are encouraged by the staff to have a significant influence on the life of the school as opposed to feeling like their lives are run by others. This research seems to suggest what real-life examples confirm:

> *Individual staff members who add most to a healthy school environment are those who persistently initiate opportunities for quality relationships outside their offices and classrooms.*

School counselors stand out as the individuals with the best training to initiate and support these efforts.

Initiators of Improvement

Counselors and teachers who want to improve school safety, morale, and achievement through a hallways approach need to ask themselves some hard personal questions to judge their potential for success. You already receive credit for the quality work you do now, and probably no one is beating down your door demanding that you do things differently. Money and awards will not come pouring at you if you attend more to hallway interactions. There are plenty of reasons why each of us would be resistant to changing the ways we work, and there is probably little official demand to fight that resistance. We need to be aware of those factors that might make us more resistant, the factors that would move us to change, and the ways they interact in the choices we make.

Counselors receive broader training in relationships, student development, student needs, and how to help people achieve maximum potential than anyone, although many teachers have also made this an area of expertise. No one has a better background for promoting more positive relationships among students, teachers, parents, administrators, and the community than counselors. We have the mission and the skills, but there are also natural pressures that force us into some difficult choices on what roles to take.

Speaking Up

It is often easier to keep your mouth shut and back away than to speak out or act in difficult situations. The trouble is that you may wind up following someone else's bad directions. The challenge is to recognize and use the informal power available to you so that you can make use of all your potential influence.

Taking Risks

There is high risk firmly attached to the importance of what you do and the satisfaction you find. Some will take safer, more stable routes by making limited choices, acting in rigid ways, and minimizing change. But the stability this creates eventually turns into boredom and dull sameness as the many burned-out professionals who go for therapy or leave the profession can attest. Positive change and growth are available in the confusing, uncertain crowds of the hallways, but they may force you to relinquish some security.

Stepping Out

What a joy it was as neophyte professionals walking into new offices, arranging the pencils, storing the pads, putting up thoughtful decorations, and aligning the seats just right. We naively expected the most amazing things would happen on an hourly basis. It didn't take long before we realized how many critical relationships were going on outside the office and that people usually take their problems to someone other than the counselor. These are the times when you make choices between developing new personal and professional relationships in unfamiliar territory or shrinking back to deal with as few people and tasks as possible.

Leading the Advance

The mantle of leadership cannot be avoided forever if you are to make the most of your talents. Sometimes it is desired, other times it is thrust on you, and occasionally you take it because there is no other acceptable alternative. The variable pressures to be follower, leader, and even hermit are what we must all recognize as part of just being human. Facing them and making the most of our abilities is what brings us the most pride in ourselves.

There are no ultimate right and wrong choices about how each of us becomes an initiator of better things for our students and schools, but the location for vibrant, new, possible actions is clear:

Reality, opportunity for change, human variety, and challenge are greatest in the hallways, playgrounds, parking lots, and streets where people are actively moving through their lives.

Just as a piano does not have a single best key or combination of keys, neither do you have one way that will always work best. The secret is in knowing as many keys and combinations as possible so that you can continually experiment with developing better and more pleasing patterns of relationships. Even the people who are as different as the sharps and flats on a piano can be arranged in the right combination with the right timing to make a positive human symphony.

The remainder of this book will provide new relationship development strategies and show you how to use some old skills in new ways. Whether you use the whole model or separate pieces to create your own personal style of helping is up to you. Either way can change the patterns of your work to better encourage a more healthy environment in and around the hallways of your school.

Making the Hallways Work for You

The starting place for successful helping is to gain an understanding of those you want to help, their issues, and the situations surrounding them. The next chapter provides easy-to-use concepts that will help you quickly assess hallway situations where you can make a difference. There is little time for slow reactions once you are in the hallways, so the ability to think in terms of a few key pieces of information becomes essential.

2

Mapping
Hallway Relationships

Parents know to follow the sign at the entry to every school: "Please report directly to the principal's office." When students are in class, the hallways are deceptively quiet and peaceful places. Then the bell rings, and the quiet corridors turn into a turmoil where parents caught out in the open hug the walls for safety. Neither the chaos and confusion of students jostling in the halls, nor the deceptive serenity when they are in the classroom, convey much about the people involved. It is the individual experiences of joy, safety, anxiety, and danger that are at the heart of hallway experiences. Consider just a couple of the examples that professionals know all too well.

At the high school, Gwenn is pregnant and hasn't told anyone, and Dwan thinks the world will collapse if he doesn't get into the "right" college. Pushing, shoving, and cursing get Dan in trouble daily when he leaves his 4th-grade classroom. Jean comes in from the playground in tears nearly every day. Mr. Adle wants the problem kids out of his 8th-grade class, and he doesn't care how it is done. Everyone wants out of Mr. Adle's class. The PTA president just had a heart attack at a critical time and the extremely shy vice president would rather quit than take the job, so she wants you to fix things for her. The realities of people's lives in the hallways would make the strongest professionals want to run away and hide, and sometimes that is just what we do.

Office Security

There is no place where I can do counseling as effectively as in my office. It provides security, isolation, time, confidentiality, structure, and control that are available nowhere else with such consistency. A good office is the perfect place for standard counseling and administrative work, a setting in which you can create a controlled detachment from the confusion of the rest of the world. But sometimes that detachment is not so controlled, and the office can become an escape mechanism.

As effective as the office can be as a relief mechanism, it can also become an addictive hiding place where life outside can be avoided. The signs of hallway avoidance may be as simple as the sinking feeling in your stomach, the increased pounding of your heart, or the deep sigh that comes when you prepare to leave the office. Perhaps it is the unexpected desire to make one more telephone call, score one more test, fill out one more form, or write one more letter of reference. As frustrating as administrative duties can be, they can also offer relief from dealing with more difficult problems waiting in the hallways.

As with any addiction, some people continuously give in to the relief opportunities and leave the real world behind as often as possible. Others reject their avoidance urges altogether and forgo important tasks to be in the middle of the hallway turmoil continuously. Most find ways to blend periods of relief with hallway turmoil in order to maintain a measure of wellness while still facing hallway realities on a regular basis.

Finding the time and energy to use and enjoy hallway relationships requires a simple, yet flexible plan to guide your efforts and provide some safety outlets when things go awry. The starting place is to determine the essential pieces of information needed to quickly decide on appropriate actions. You have already proven your counseling skills, so this plan should put you in a position to implement those skills quickly, in more places, more often.

The counseling office allows time for evaluating students, which issues are most important, how much time the students have, and even which techniques you will use. Gaining an understanding of people and situations is just as important in preparation to helping in the hallways—and the starting place is to realize your own goals and limitations.

Limited Time Equals Limited Goals

Hallway helping does not have the luxury of 1 hour each week or more that standard counseling can offer. What you can do in 1 to 5 minutes in a crowd is not what you can do in a private office hour. To be successful in hallway helping, your actions will have to reflect the limitations of this approach while emphasizing its unique strengths.

Life is a series of growth experiences that will be given quality attention, poor attention, or no attention by individuals and others in their environment. People who experience quality development throughout life get maximum positive attention for the best of their actions. When little positive attention is given to the same potentially valuable actions, people will not make the best use of their life experiences. The need for productive attention exists throughout each day, and it must come quickly and regularly to be effective. Hallway helping at its best provides for the numerous brief interactions needed to reinforce positive happenings in a person's life and to communicate short bursts of support when people need a lift.

Working out the details of difficult situations, taking an in-depth look at oneself, walking through a decision-making process, and doing extensive problem solving are not goals for hallway interactions. The time and confidentiality needed for these demanding goals are usually only available in the counseling office. Hallway goals are those that fill in the practical gaps for these larger goals. What hallway goals can accomplish are recognizing when one is in a difficult situation; verifying times when a new understanding of one's self is demonstrated; providing immediate support for a good decision or recognition that another decision didn't work; and encouraging practice of problem-solving techniques in the real world.

The overall goal for hallway helping is to provide numerous, brief, personalized, and targeted interactions as regularly as possible to as many people as possible.

All counseling theories tell us that people need to recognize and be regularly reminded of the difference between the productive and nonproductive aspects of their lives. Chaos theory tells us that even the smallest, seemingly insignificant actions, when combined with other factors in a person's environment, can turn out to make a greater difference over time than any one major directed action. The essence of hallway helping combines these recognition, reminding, and reality factors with the willingness to make continuous small differences in peoples' lives. The long-term life goals can still be great, but the hallway helper must focus on smaller goals in order to recognize their value and the progress being made. The limitations associated with these goals make it imperative that the hallway helper focus on only the most essential factors about a person and her situation so that helpful actions can be taken as quickly and as frequently as possible.

Matching Contexts

The first step toward entering hallway relationships is to recognize the immediate situations of those you contact. Gwenn is young, unmarried, in school, and pregnant. How you deal with her issues should be far different from how you approach Dan's aggressiveness, Mr. Adle's desire to have the problem students removed from his class, or the PTA vice president's shyness. Whether needs are of a personal, social, or professional nature should influence what interventions you try, as well as where, when, and how you use them. The faster you can match what you say and do to the other person's context, the more likely you will be to have a productive hallway relationship.

Personal Context

Students often need to do intrapersonal processing of thoughts, feelings, and choices before they share them with others or take direct action. This personal context requires clarification of one's individual needs, beliefs, desires, and goals, and generally deserves the isolation and time provided by the counseling office. Brief hallway interventions become more valuable as highly personal issues begin to display themselves in public arenas and take on a more social nature.

Gwenn's unwanted and unexpected pregnancy is a personal issue of major proportions. Exploring her feelings about it, considering her options, breaking the news to her parents, discussing possibilities with the father-to-be, and what it will mean to her life are critical personal issues that need to be discussed quickly, thoughtfully, and in private. Only after she has her thoughts, emotions, and reasoning more firmly together will the hallways become appropriate for the more social context of work with parents, friends, and boyfriend.

Social Context

Many times, students understand what they need to do and already have the skills or ability to implement necessary changes. Problems in a social context involve students practicing in the real world and with real people what they know in their heads or can put into words but have trouble implementing in real life. This is an ideal context for hallway helping.

Dan is bigger than the other kids, and his pushing and shoving outside the classroom make him feel powerful and in control. Talking to Dan in an office is not likely to make much of a dent in his perceptions of how to deal with people or how they react to him. Short interventions with Dan in the hallways have the advantage of directly attending to the issues of power and control in the actual social context where real people and real reactions are immediately available.

The PTA vice president provides a very different example of how the concept of hallway helping can be expanded beyond the literal hallways of schools. She is a mature and competent woman with hesitancies about being in the public eye. What she needs most is to practice her abilities by being encouraged, supported, and having her value recognized in public. Professionals who help her move into those situations with the necessary support provided both immediately and afterwards are the ones who can turn a seemingly unrelated situation into one that influences students, administrators, and parents throughout the community.

Professional Context

Many student, parent, and teacher issues relate to the professional or academic context of the school. This academic emphasis revolves around student reading, clarifying, relating, and recalling. They include discussions of scheduling, program planning, career exploration, and interviewing for work. These issues require that attention first be given to the person's formal role within the school community (student, counselor, teacher, administrator, committee member, etc.) with personal and social contexts temporarily given a secondary status.

Dwan wants desperately to get into a college as soon as possible. This need falls first into the professional context. Matching his student context with your role as knowledgeable and helpful professional can be easily done in the hallways and need not start in a 40-minute office session. Casual comments and brief discussions can give Dwan much to think about, resources to find, direct actions to take, and things to talk about with others. Numerous informal interactions on a regular basis will increase the professional and personal bonds between the two of you as well as his knowledge base.

Mr. Adle provides a very different example of a useful professional context. His desire to remove students from class at any cost is not the norm, but it is also not unique. You know his reactions are not all professional and that numerous personal and social issues are probably involved. Unfortunately, the personal and social issues are not likely to be the ones you come in contact with first from Mr. Adle. It is more likely that he will stop you in the teacher's lounge and tell you what needs to be done to whom in no uncertain terms. Because he is approaching you in a strictly professional context, the best way to begin dealing with him is to match that context. Thoughtful listening to his concerns, demands, and consideration of rules, roles, and regulations is the best starting place for a relationship that could become productive. Challenging him immediately might satisfy your personal frustration, but being patient will set a more productive stage for a future helping relationship.

Determining whether someone is initially coming to you in a personal, social, or professional context will be the first clue about how to proceed. Once you know something of where the person or group is coming from, then you can begin to consider other conditions affecting the timing, place, and style of your hallway relationship.

Timing

Time waits for no one, but life continues even when someone is in a hurry. Dwan is a worrier and wants to decide what college he will attend by the end of this, his sophomore year. Mr. Adle is demanding "those damn kids" be out of his class immediately, but that request will fall on deaf ears. Gwenn will have to wait 7 months before the baby is born, but in a few weeks the pregnancy will show and decisions will then need to be made quickly. Some of these problems have plenty of time for casual approaches, short hallway approaches, whereas others require more immediacy and formal attention. Your job is to recognize the differences so that your actions can match the timing needs.

Judging the true time pressure on an individual is necessary to choose the best individual helping strategy. This may seem like an obvious idea, but when problems, people, and ideas are coming at you from all directions, panic and mistakes become commonplace. In the hallways, you need a simple triage plan similar in concept to those used in a hospital emergency room. You sort problems by priorities based how quickly things need to be handled and how much survival is an issue.

Now or Never

Now-or-never situations leave no recourse other than to drop everything and act immediately, or the moment to act will have vanished. Examples might be breaking up a fight where one person is in danger, giving quick advice to a teacher with an angry parent waiting in the office, or consoling a child who has just found out his mother died in a car accident. Miss the opportunity to act immediately in situations like this and you will have missed the chance to have a major impact.

Little to no preparation or planning are present for these now-or-never situations. These are instances when you must have confidence in your professional reactions so that no time is lost. Quick consultations, definitive actions, and continual evaluation of how well your intervention is working are the keys to any interventions you try in this timing situation. Recognizing when the emergency is over is also important so that you can consider other less hurried interventions.

Pressured

Pressured situations require decisions to be made in a limited amount of time and have significant consequences if the decisions are not made appropriately. They usually require relatively quick action or at least discussion of current actions. Gwenn's unexpected pregnancy is a very difficult situation, and in her mind it will certainly feel like a now-or-never situation. The situation is actually not quite the now-or-never situation she fears, because there are months before the baby is due, weeks to decide how to tell the general community, and at least days to prepare for telling her parents. Gwenn has time to talk, think, and plan even though she must make some decisions very soon. You can take your time and act less directly in more situations than most people would expect.

Casual

There is plenty of time to talk, think, reflect, and plan in a casual situation, but it is important that such activities go on regularly. My daughter Shannon was an excellent 1st-grade student who was panicked the first time she missed several questions on a homework assignment. She was sure that she was failing and would never catch up. To her this was a major emergency, and certainly we attended to her anxiety. But the most important actions we took were those that attended to the developmental nature of her experience. Talking about the situation, getting her to talk with the teacher, demonstrating our own mistakes, making sure she saw our confidence in her, and considering ways we could check to see that things were going well in the future were the critical actions we took to emphasize the actual casual-timing situation. This is a classic situation for future focused hallway strategies that can be offered quickly and regularly to build and maintain confidence.

Long Term

The essence of a long-term strategy is preparation for serious discussions about action, rather than directly taking action. Mr. Adle believes he is in a now-or-never situation, and in some sense he may be correct. He probably needs to find someone to blow off steam to or everyone is likely to suffer. Once the steam is blown off, this becomes a long-term situation. The task is to say and do things that will calm, support, and build a relationship base designed to promote growth in the future. This type of situation has been a long time building, and you cannot reverse it in one short burst of counseling brilliance.

Timing is crucial in building productive relationships outside the office cocoon, but there is more to it than timing alone. Seemingly good timing must also be used in the right place to be effective.

Location

Many of you will identify with the first time I had to administer a standardized test. Where else could I administer a test to a large group except in the cafeteria? It was all so logical until I realized that cooks talk, laugh, and bang pans. And if the noise wasn't enough, the smell of fresh rolls and lasagna started permeating the room after the test had begun. Stomachs grumbled, heads began looking up, and students started resting their heads on the tests. Eyes blinked closed, some looked to the ceiling, and students increasingly wanted to go to the bathroom. The cafeteria was a great place for lunch, but a lousy place to give a test.

Location is important, but know that there is no one best place for hallway helping. Depending on what you need to get done, who you must do it with, and when it needs to happen, there will always be places that provide better opportunities than others. Innumerable specifics might help determine the ultimate meeting place for a given situation, but who would remember them all? A basic decision between private versus public and between quiet versus noisy will give you a solid start that can usually be adjusted later.

Private Versus Public

The classes you had in graduate school directed you to meet clients with as much privacy as possible. Helping in the hallways requires another way of thinking that emphasizes the value of having others around.

Gwenn is dealing with critical life issues and is very upset about them. Her most pressing concerns call for highly private and confidential settings, but she needs additional settings as well. For example, she needs practice dealing with feelings of embarrassment over her situation. She needs support and affirmation for her efforts.

After telling you about her situation, Gwenn will be looking hard to see how you react to her outside the office. Although the thoughts running through her mind in the office will be on herself, seeing you in the hallways will focus attention on your reactions as tests of how others might react in the future:

- "Will she treat me differently now that I've told her?"
- "Will she be angry?"
- "Will she show caring like she always does, or not because I'm pregnant?"
- "Will her different attention be an embarrassment or a good feeling? Will it be OK, or will I want to run away?"

The place to get these questions answered is in the hallways, where the real world conveys a special brand of truth and understanding. Hallways are the places for public words and actions; things that others can see or hear. One of the worst things you can do is to try to bring your highly private office relationship into the hallways. Words and actions that show others you know something very new and different about Gwenn will do her no favors.

Hallway actions and words are best used to test ideas in the real world that have already been thought through in more private settings.

Some hallway interactions require more privacy than others. Mr. Adle may need to be guided from the middle of the hallway to a corner, where his anger will receive less negative attention. When Jean is in tears from being teased in the hallways, a quiet walk out around the empty playground might be just the ticket to help her regain control before going back to class. Hallways are not private places, but there are degrees of privacy that can be achieved if you use all the locations available. They can add a public dimension to your interventions that emphasize social interactions and experiential learning in multiple locations.

Quiet Versus Loud

Everybody knows why you want quiet, but why would you ever want noise in a helping relationship? The textbooks offer no answers here, but an evening at a rowdy basketball game will shed some light. Emotions and reactions take over in their most raw forms. People who are quiet the rest of the day yell and scream things that will come out nowhere else. They are excited and involved, and their natural emotions and strengths take over from the self-doubts controlling them the rest of the day. For many people, it is the rigid structure they place on most of their ordered lives that keeps them from growing and learning about other exciting potentials in themselves. Noise and excitement help break that rigidity down and allow hidden aspects of a person to come into play.

Noisy places can provide relief for people in situations like Gwenn's. She can casually avoid personal conversations because of the noise, but the noise will force her to be close to people in order to be heard. The closeness in crowded and noisy hallways can be threatening, but it can also be comforting when someone needs physical closeness that is not easily asked for or given. As a male counselor, I can walk in crowded hallways next to a female student, even brushing our arms together in a show of support with much less attention than if we were standing alone or entering my office. The same is even more true for many male students who might otherwise never allow themselves to be seen physically touching another male. Noisy hallways, dances, gyms, and playgrounds are places where people are forced to be close with minimal stigma attached. These can be just the settings that create readiness for change.

Readiness

One of our greatest frustrations is seeing clearly what people need to do yet not being able to get them to act. Dan wants to be liked but only knows how to impress other children with aggressive behaviors. Gwenn obviously needs to begin working things out with her mother and father as quickly as possible, but she is stopped by fear. These students display different degrees of readiness to work on their issues, which affects what hallway or counseling office strategies will work best for each. How willing someone is to work and the abilities they have to get the work done are the key readiness ingredients.

Willingness is the degree to which a person has sufficient interpersonal motivation and confidence to succeed at a relationship task. The more willingness that is present, the greater will be the potential for an assertive approach and a successful outcome. The absence of willingness results in no situation being small enough to handle, no idea easy enough to grasp, and no amount of ability sufficient for success.

When someone's tension level is high enough, there will be no willingness to act regardless of the value of taking action or how skilled at helping you may be. Having patience is the key at high tension levels. At moderate tension levels, *anxiety* is present in sufficient amounts to raise concerns, while still allowing movement toward action. These are probably the most productive levels for helping. *Confidence* describes a low tension level where actions are taken without much thought of the consequences, so here you need to be most cautious with suggestions. *Abilities* are the interpersonal information and skills brought to a relationship task. For most purposes, you can decide that a person will be either "able" or "unable" to deal with the nature and difficulty level of a specific relationship task. Only when a person brings the necessary abilities to the task or learns them during the relationship can that relationship be productive for everyone involved.

Willingness and ability factors combine to influence the ways you must act in order to be successful. A lack of ability in the area of social relationships is Dan's greatest problem. He would like to have better relationships with his peers (willingness), but he doesn't have confidence in any of his skills other than to be inappropriately aggressive. Hallway interactions with Dan can focus on modeling appropriate social skills, short circuiting potentially inappropriate behaviors, and showing support for productive social behaviors.

Gwenn is at a moderate to high anxiety level of willingness where she is very worried but can still recognize the requirement to act. She has plenty of relationship ability to begin dealing with the situation and just enough willingness to take some initial actions. This knowledge allows you to plan for movement from work in the counseling office to affirming actions in the hallways and at home. Keeping in mind the context, timing, and readiness aspects of a situation will help you quickly choose quality actions in the rapidly changing circumstances of hallway interactions.

Charting a Hallway Course

Information doesn't do anyone much good unless it fits into some organized picture. My wife always beats me at trivia games because she has many more efficient ways of organizing random facts. Factual knowledge only comes out for me when I am in the middle of a discussion, reading, or writing something that follows a simple and

TABLE 2.1 Hallway Assessments

Context	(What are the issues?)
____ Personal	
____ Social	
____ Professional	
Timing	(How much should I hurry?)
____ Now or Never	
____ Pressured	
____ Casual	
____ Long-term	
Location	(Where should things occur?)
____ Private versus Public	
____ Quiet versus Loud	
Readiness	(How much preparation is needed?)
Willingness	
____ rejection	
____ anxiety	
____ confidence	
Ability	
____ able	
____ unable	

logical pattern of thought. Table 2.1 provides the framework of the ideas used for deciding where, when, and how to negotiate hallway relationships. Some will think through interactions they know will arise and review recent experiences to see how they did. The most organized may keep notes on people or situations, while others will only maintain a rough outline in their heads. Your task is to make use of the framework in the formal or informal ways that fit you best.

The next chapter offers a set of steps to move from this evaluation of the hazards and potentials to the direct actions needed to follow through on your assessment.

3

Quick Steps to Success

For all the work I do with counselors, teachers, parents, and administrators, it is student interactions outside the classroom that provide me with the greatest dose of humility. I love the work and get plenty of reinforcement, but still, the second-guessing starts for me on the drive home. "Did I have enough control of the situation or maybe I should have done something more?" "What took me so long to act?" "How could I forget something I'd done hundreds of times?" "What in the world caused me to say that?" "Did that student think I ignored her?" I may have had years of successful interactions with students, but I still have those all too human symptoms of forgetting, missing a cue, stuttering, or taking actions that I'd like to change later. Reviewing the brief set of steps in this chapter as reminders of things I already know helps me keep on track, even if they don't cure all my human weaknesses.

Understanding the lives of people in the hallways has little value until you turn that knowledge into action. A solid plan for taking quick, appropriate action, evaluating the results, and deciding what to do next can provide the direction and confidence needed to do the best job possible. The brevity and frequency of hallway interventions requires a plan that lets you immediately tap into the skills and knowledge your training and experiences have already provided. The demand for reflexive action in the hallways is similar to increasing pressures being felt throughout the business and the counseling fields. These are the pressures that have brought business to *The One-Minute Manager* (Blanchard & Johnson, 1982), whereas *Single Session Therapy* (Talmon, 1990) and *Brief Counseling That Works* (Sklare, 1997) continue to influence the counseling profession. Each of these models offers similar general guidelines: Gain control of the situation, relate immediately, set limited goals, support strengths, move quickly to action, continuously reassess, and finish what you can before you lose your client. These are guidelines that work, and the following steps will help you adapt these brief intervention concepts to hallway settings.

Now that you realize both Gwenn's immediate and long-range needs, which do you deal with in the hallway? How do you reduce Dwan's dependence on you and increase self-reliance? What can be done to get the kids to stop picking on Jean? Can Dan be taught how to be assertive rather than aggressive? Is there a way to quickly move the PTA vice president from isolation and panic to being effective in a group? Wishing Mr. Adle away is not likely to work, so how do you make him easier for everyone to live with for the time being? The starting place in each case is to first bring as much stability as possible to the situation so your knowledge and skills will have the opportunity to make a difference.

Step 1: Stabilize the Situation

Every relationship requires some level of safety and security to ensure that learning takes place. Whether it is the office, classroom, or the much less predictable hallways and gymnasiums, some sense of stability is essential.

The first goal is to gain just enough control of the situation so that those who would help have the opportunity to do so and those in need can recognize and accept the help being offered.

When Dan is punching out another student, remember to put your best counseling skills on hold for a while. The first action is to de-escalate the situation and bring the official rules and personnel into action. Listening, reasoning, and understanding will be effective at a later time, after safety and security are reestablished.

Subtlety is worthless when the situation is out of control. This is a time to make use of the system with its defined roles and rules to gain and maintain a semblance of order. Remind yourself of the following guidelines for making the best use of all that is available to you. These guidelines are not complex, but they are easy to forget:

- Gaining control by force and demanding behaviors are usually harmful for long-range benefits but sometimes essential if enough danger is present. Shoot for long-range benefits by using less force and fewer demands as danger levels decrease.
- Use the official rules to help you gain control. Discounting rules is legally problematic and justifies rule-ignoring behaviors on the part of others. Work on changing poor rules formally *after* the emergency has passed.
- Encourage everyone to carry out his or her official responsibilities. Usurping the rightful role of the student, principal, teacher, parent, police officer, and so forth because you think you can do it better robs those individuals of power. They are then likely to either abdicate their roles altogether or fight you.
- Convey the message that there will be a time later to deal with everyone's concerns. Right now the only need is to "get under control."
- Communicate accurate tension levels. You may need to calm some people, whereas others will need their anxiety levels raised to match the realities of the situation.
- Delay decisions about the future. Poor decisions are made when emotions are high and events are out of control.

Gaining control of the situation and helping others get a grip is the essential foundation for helping. Logical reasoning never wins out in the middle of a screaming argument. Only after the situational bleeding is stopped can you begin preparing relationships for growth and renewal.

Step 2: Build Multiple Relationships

The major benefit of working in the hallways is direct access to the people and reality, so your goal is to recognize and effectively involve as many people as possible as realistically as possible. Some people will be useful in hallway helping immediately and others might be harmful at one time but essential later.

The objective in this early stage is to encourage multiple relationship-building actions and minimize those that reduce the chances of building positive relationships.

Consider Mr. Adle in the hallway exchanging defiant glances with three students. Although nothing direct is happening, tension is obvious, and you know there have been problems brewing. Other students are giving them a wide birth and walk by with eyes averted. The absence of clear and immediate conflict allows you to work on building multiple relationships for the future rather than directly dealing with confrontation.

This is not the time for brilliant therapeutic interventions but instead for some solid interactions that are not new to you but that might easily be forgotten. For example, you might approach the boys casually and speak to a positive aspect of a hallway relationship you have developed, "Sorry you didn't get to the career day planning meeting the other day. I think your ideas would have been appreciated. We're having another meeting next week. Can we get you to come?" You might also find a way to say something casual to Mr. Adle as you pass him: "Long week already, and it's only Tuesday."

These brief hallway exchanges are not designed to put a stop to a brewing conflict nor to make anyone a model citizen. Instead, long-

term relationship building is emphasized to create multiple founda-
tions for future work. Consider some of the benefits of remembering
to use your skills in these casual ways:

- You demonstrate the value of positive interactions in the midst
  of threatening circumstances and suspect relationships.

- You model for bystanders that it is worthwhile to approach
  difficult people during tense situations and possible to lower
  tension levels at the same time.

- You give individuals recognition that is desired but not always
  offered in casual situations.

- Your casual approach downplays concerns, lowers tension levels, and changes the focus to a more positive direction.

- You communicate through your actions belief in the positive
  value of all the individuals.

Increasing the number and quality of relationships that can be
used either immediately or at a later time is a key move toward
maximizing the long-term potential of hallway helping. Building an
ever-widening support system is crucial for developing a healthy
community atmosphere in which all individuals and groups are
given personal recognition and attention. The more people that can
be moved to feel this way, the easier it will be to actually meet the
needs of individuals.

Step 3: Clarify Contexts

Identifying individual needs and the contexts in which you ought
to work with them are essential. This is where the context of the
person's problem (personal, social, or professional) is taken into
consideration. The stability and community building of the first two
steps set the stage to select the interventions you can best provide.

Professional training most directly prepared you for this step that
emphasizes observing, listening, thinking, and focusing on the individual in need. Dwan wants you to take the responsibility of finding

him the right college and ensuring his success at getting in. This step is the one in which you decide whether your actions will be guided by following his stated directions, "find me a school," or by attending to his avoidance of immediate responsibilities and directly facing self-confidence issues. The "finding a school" issue sounds like a professional context, whereas the responsibility and self-confidence issues are more personal and social. Which of these contexts you will first give attention to is the decision.

An individual who is much more likely to have his needs ignored to the detriment of himself and those around him is Mr. Adle. As much as you may dislike him, this is the point where you need to recognize him as an individual with his own set of personal, social, and professional problems that could benefit from your attention. A decision to disregard his needs would be easy in comparison with Gwenn's pregnancy, Jean's victimization, or even Dwan's anxieties. Some might use his professional status as an excuse to ignore his needs, "He ought to act more professional and do what he is paid to do. He deserves what he gets"; or administration could be blamed for not altering his behavior. In fact, Mr. Adle's demanding, loud, self-serving, and obnoxious behaviors will probably drive most people away, which is how he confirms that others don't care about him.

The task of fighting through Mr. Adle's exterior to find ways of meeting his individual needs is one most of us would actively avoid if given the choice. But this is still a person who directly affects the students and adults around him on a daily basis. The road to helping them goes at least partially through Mr. Adle, so that avoiding his needs makes our work with others more difficult. Attending to his needs in conjunction with the goals of others can improve the relationships and success of everyone in the school.

Step 4: Establish Common Goals

Helping in the hallways seeks to blend the goals of two or more people into one concerted effort. A 7th-grade girl may want to spend more time with friends in order to make herself feel more accepted, whereas a supportive teacher might see her need to spend more time on homework and study that will better secure her future. These two could develop a conflict-ridden relationship if they continue to focus on their disparate goals. If, however, they can be helped to reach agreement on a goal in common, such as developing joint student projects or group study techniques, they will have the basis for a helpful and productive relationship.

Finding common goals among people in the hallways and identifying 30-second interactions to encourage them lets you spread out your effectiveness and use more of the available positive resources. The more you know about the strengths, weaknesses, hopes, and dreams of the people around you the better you will be able to establish and make use of such common goals. The secret is to keep those goals modest and achievable. Encouraging people to spend their life working for world peace may be laudable, but helping them say something peaceful to a person they don't like is a much more achievable first step. Modest goals, achieved in a small step-by-small step fashion, are the model for finding hallway success.

Dwan wants to get accepted to a college and be away from everyone here as soon as possible. You feel that what he really needs is to gain a better understanding of himself and the world by interacting with more students. Matching Dwan's perceived goal with yours might be done by first finding other students with complementary goals to Dwan's. For example, it is reasonable to expect that Dwan will have a friend (Ted) who thinks in similar ways and that both of them might be very weak in developing peer relationships. If you can get Ted working on the goal of developing better peer relationships, then your potential to influence Dwan increases dramatically. The closer the three of you can get to common formal or unstated goals, modest in nature, the more progress is likely to occur for Dwan, Ted, and others they might touch.

Gwenn too would benefit from developing common goals related to her pregnancy with her parents, her teachers, and even her friends in order for these relationships to become more supportive. These are not the fake commonalities often expressed as, "Whatever you want, we'll be here for you" and "We're behind you all the way." Well meaning as these may be, they don't reflect the necessary joint goals of a quality relationship that normally require negotiations of differing individual needs.

Publicly confirming common goals worked out elsewhere is a perfect role for hallway relationships. For example, as Gwenn's friends become involved in her advancing pregnancy, you might recognize efforts to improve their eating habits for the baby: "It looks like you are all eating a little healthier nowadays." The identification and strengthening of common goals is essential if you are to go on to more direct actions with confidence that they will work for you.

Step 5: Select Actions Pragmatically

The most effective ways you have found to help others in the past will come into play now. One counselor told me that after a series of hallway interactions she counted at least five different theories she had partially used. She saw a rational emotive flavor at times, took behavioral actions to reduce inappropriate behaviors, and the Adlerian in her kept trying to understand the whole picture. Most of you will start by being attentive and then choose different directions guided by what has worked best in the past. Theory that served you well before will also have value in hallway interactions. Just keep in mind that the practical value of your actions will be determined by which verbal, physical, and social strategies will be most appropriate.

Verbal strategies are the ones given most attention in counselor and teacher training. What to say, when to say it, and how to say it are critical issues in any orientation. How you choose your words for counseling or teaching will not change so much in your hallway helping, but the ways you use them must change.

The calm, quiet, encouraging voice used effectively in the office will be lost in the hallways, at a dance, or at the basketball game. There are no verbal alternatives in these situations: You either get louder and more aggressive or you give up on verbal skills. Dictating a quiet atmosphere in the hallways is not possible, so you must adjust to what is there.

The pragmatic verbal changes you make require more flexibility rather than learning anything specifically new. Switching from speaking softly in close, tense situations to being loud in crowded, noisy situations is a major change, because everyone has clear preferences in this area. It is no small task learning to express all you want effectively in a few chopped words in a crowd rather than using the elaborately clear explanations you can provide in an office. And emotions such as excitement, joy, frustration, and sadness need to be exaggerated in crowds well beyond the subtle differences we can communicate in private. This required verbal flexibility also demands that you make matching physical changes to be effective.

The *physical* strategies you choose for hallways demand greater variety and practice than those that work in the office. Communicating different levels of trust, attention, objectivity, and so forth in the office is all done from basically the same sitting position with minimal movement. Adjusting to the complex movements required in the hallways is no easy matter. Even the simple act of conversing while walking down the hall demands a great deal of coordination.

Mobile hallway conversations can be quite laughable when you think of all that must actually be accomplished at once. Walk at just the right speed so as not to step on someone in front or get run over from the back; match your stride to your conversational partner; watch where you are going; maintain eye contact; recognize, consider, and decide how to use other people who might be listening; have a goal for the conversation; and last but not least, speak intelligibly. A few choreography lessons might be in order for even the most graceful among us.

Closeness and touch are the most sensitive physical differences between hallway helping and office counseling or classroom teaching. The formality of the office or classroom provides consistent rules for physical closeness that are not available in less formal situations. Adjustments come in many forms as the following samples demonstrate:

- Giving physical signals is more important in hallways because of all the turmoil.
- Simply being present can convey tremendous caring.
- Your smile may be the only one someone recognizes all day.
- A brief squeeze on the shoulder may be the only available way to effectively communicate, "I care, and you're not alone."
- A little harder squeeze might also say, "Don't do what you are thinking," and get it said in the privacy of silence.

Ethical guidelines avoid the area of touching and distance outside the office because the rules are so vague. Greater exaggeration and wider variation of behaviors required for hallway conditions do not lend themselves to clean, safe, and specific rules. Whether hallway behaviors are ethical or not will most often be judged on loosely constructed social mores rather than by regulations. This makes it critical that you understand the social guidelines in your community, the degree of their flexibility, and how to use these social factors to your advantage.

Social strategies are the arrangements you make to facilitate the interactions of others. These are situations created to bring people together or keep them apart in order to promote productive social interactions. Only the most naive social do-gooder would see angry people in the hallway and suggest they "get together after school and make friends." Effective social action in this case encourages angry individuals and groups to temporarily remain separated in order to reduce tension levels. Appropriately changing social conditions can reduce tension and buy time for future progress under healthier circumstances.

Dwan's situation is not a dangerous one, but it would benefit from more social contact. You might ask him to meet you in places where your interactions can lead to other relationships. Those places are in the hallways, the cafeteria, and the local hangout where people you want him to meet congregate regularly. You might find that Mr. Adle runs the chess club, which is the one place at school where he is liked. Getting more people involved with him in the club environment or increasing the chess club's involvement with other school or community groups are examples of positive social strategies for building relationships. In each case, you are trying to arrange social situations that will bring the right people together under optimal conditions for the greatest overall good.

Step 6: Multiply Connections

A key advantage that hallways have over your office is the availability of many more sources of information, feedback, action, and reinforcements. Using these multiple resources to help only one person at a time as you might well do in the office is a poor use of hallway potential. The dynamic mix of people and the vibrant nature of hallway life work best when a maximum number of people and needs are met at once. Continually seeking ways to have multiple needs met by the interactions you facilitate is always a preferred hallway strategy.

Dwan needs more social interactions and some reality checks on school and college, as well as the information he wants regarding picking a college. Matching him with Ted, who has similar as well as different needs, was a step in the right direction. Finding ways to encourage their communication with juniors and seniors would increase social and reality connections for both boys as well as help them gain information. Your knowledge of all the students will help identify the ones who could use the ego bolstering, additional relationships, nonpressured practice at helping others, and social skill development that would come while helping Dwan and Ted.

Making hallway connections between Dwan, Ted, and older students is best served by small, subtle interventions. Being in the hallways on a regular basis gives you multiple opportunities for creating casual interactions that would go unnoticed if you were not out there every day. Consider, for example, that between first and second periods Dwan and Ted are on the other side of the school from two juniors you want them to meet, but just before lunch they are in rooms next door to each other. The clear choice for a subtle intervention would be the natural meeting place and time just prior to lunch. You might purposely meet with the juniors at that time for some casual conversation and take advantage of calling Dwan and Ted over when they appear: "Hey come over here a minute. . . . You know these guys (the juniors) have been picking colleges for months, and you could learn from them. Hey, I got to run. Let me know how it goes."

This situation is promoting connections between people who all have the chance to get their personal needs met at the same time they help meet the needs of others. Emphasizing mutual benefits and multiple opportunities increases the likelihood that any intervention will succeed. Taking the formal, "let's all get together in my office" out of the equation encourages a more natural environment for peer relationships to develop. Finally, you can physically leave the situation to the students, which would be out of place in the office but absolutely expected in hallway interventions. You leave the boys with ideas, connections, encouragement, and methods to explore each other in the realities of their hallway lives.

I don't live in a fairy-tale land any more than you do, so we know that any single interaction like this is as likely to go nowhere as to have a major effect. That's one reason why many professionals stop trying or quit in frustration. What they forget is that the more interactions you effectively promote, the greater the expectations, the possibilities, and the potential for growth. Even in the worst-case scenario you gain.

Making multiple connections in the world outside the classroom is the best possible use of the environment, the people, and your own time, energy, and skills. The results can be as quick as seeing people get numerous needs met immediately or as subtle as realizing that one, virtually unnoticed step toward a more productive relationship has been taken. Dealing with multiple connections will also help you guard against personal burnout and promote work satisfaction. The more people whose lives you are consciously dealing with, the more successes you are likely to see and the better you will feel about how you use your time.

Changing people and their environment is the long-range goal, and you will get frustrated if you try to hurry results along too quickly. Change based on subtle influences, overcoming resistance, undermining entrenched negativism, and molding an environment rather than one individual will not get done in a day. Patience, flexibility, and trust in the recognition that good things develop in small steps are ideas you will have to lean on in times of frustration. But the time it takes for large-scale changes to be realized provides bonuses as well as headaches. Time offers you the opportunity to try and fail, revise your efforts, and try again without feeling like every single action you take will make or break a life.

Step 7: Adapt Based on Results

There are only two things that create a need for adapting your actions: failure and success. Failure on your part to do the right thing, failure on the student's part to progress, failure of the system to work, or various combinations are threats that should push you to continually evaluate outcomes and redesign efforts. Your chosen profession is helping people, and failing at that strikes at your personal and professional heart. Recognizing failures and weaknesses provides an impetus to reconsider actions and search for better alternatives. Not recognizing failures or ignoring them dooms you to similar failures over and over again. The result is that every training program warns of things going wrong, shows you how to recognize them, and teaches how to make corrections.

If failure is a recognized reason for making adaptations based on results, many fewer people place the same emphasis on how success also requires adaptations. Any intervention that produces positive results produces change along with it, and when change occurs, reassessment and redesign of efforts are necessary to match the new circumstances. The greater the success, the more we need to redesign and alter our efforts.

It is just as incumbent on us to evaluate and adapt after successful efforts as it is to change our strategies based on failed attempts.

Consider these reassessment and redesign needs in the context of possible interventions with Gwenn, who now wants to tell you all about her successful conversations with her mother about her pregnancy. Her mother was distraught but eventually understanding, and together they began planning for the future. The success in one situation will now change the set of goals Gwenn must face. Some long-term goals such as planning for the birth and school after the baby is born become increasingly timely. Other short-term goals like informing the father-to-be, her friends, and then the whole school will need more immediate, but only temporary action. These changing goals require new skills, revised relationships, and the ability to deal with constantly changing demands. Your key task is to continually revise hallway strategies and not get locked into those that worked in the first successful situation.

It is also possible that Gwenn's interactions with her mother could have gone poorly or that she could have hidden away until more problems arose. I have learned from working with teenage pregnancies that, although the general fears and needs may be similar, my interactions and techniques need to be very different with each situation. What worked for one young woman seemed to be of no value with another, and I never knew just what would work until the first attempt was made. Only after trying one reasonable tactic, watching how things worked or didn't work, and then adjusting my next effort to fit the results did I finally make real progress.

Productive reassessment and redesign of hallway efforts requires the use of the resources available from multiple sources. Some information will come from words as people describe how they met or didn't meet goals, were hurt, or were supported. Other information will come from visual clues of posture, facial expressions, and other physical reactions. Still more comes from your own reactions as frustration, excitement, disappointment, or elation are clues about what you may be experiencing emotionally but not cognitively. Only through the use of all these sources together are the best of your helping abilities realized.

The interactive nature of hallway relationships requires that solid evaluations and adaptations look to the total environment for information. Watching how others respond when one child abuses another tells you about available levels of fear, concern for human suffering, coping strategies, and ability to unite for a common cause. How a child's relationship with his mother is changing offers clues about what you can expect from her. How Gwenn is treated by her friends when she is around versus how they discuss her when she is not tells much more than Gwenn's words and emotions alone. Each piece of information adds to your understanding of how strategies are working and offers directions on how to revise your actions as the situation demands.

Step 8: Step Aside

Successful relationships can become addictive for experienced professionals and students alike. It feels good to help and to be helped; to love and to be loved; to appreciate and to be appreciated; to support and to be supported; and to be successful with someone or some group. All these good feelings make it hard to let go when the student's need becomes one of independence from you, as it eventually must. It is even harder when students want to hold on and your job becomes one of forcefully pushing them into less secure relationships.

One benefit of hallway relationships is that they produce less obvious individual contact and influence than traditional counseling relationships, which makes letting go easier. You are never quite sure what brought about good results. How does anyone know for sure whether the critical support and influence Jean needed to overcome her victim status came from you or the people and situations you helped facilitate? Did you temporarily lower tension levels that calmed Dan's temper down, or would it have happened by itself? Did Gwenn's interactions with her mother go well because of your influence or because of Gwenn and her mother's own abilities and motivations? Did Dwan's new relationships really come from you or were they bound to happen all along? The better you become as a hallway helper, the more you will spread around the apparent responsibility for change and encourage positive independence. The most effective hallway helpers might even wind up asking themselves, "Did anyone even recognize what damn good work I did?"

The student who clings to you may make you feel important, but that should not be confused with success. The overattached student is uncomfortable with other normal student relationships, and your ethical responsibilities direct you to increase those other relationships and decrease your own. The overattached professional is usually one who has seen real progress, gets confirmation from the student, and enjoys the interactions, thereby preferring more contact rather than working harder to decrease contact. The ethical concern of putting the student's needs before your own becomes the key issue. Both cases point up the need to develop natural sources of support within the hallway environment and continually push others to use those sources.

Hallway helping is not a random set of actions. Effectiveness over time is achieved by employing a consistent pattern of decision making, action, evaluation, and adaptation. This basic action model can then be used to deal with a variety of students and adults in numerous situations. Students are, of course, the group that should receive the most attention from hallway helpers, and the specific tactics found to be most useful with them are presented in the next chapter.

4

Captive Clients

The last job I held before becoming a school counselor was counseling in a prison. It was better preparation for being a school counselor than I ever expected. School is not the prison that some people call it, but there are many important similarities between the two environments that work in the favor of those who want to help. Prisoners and students both have required places to be during the day, specific rules to follow, and continuous direction and supervision. Learning to use the characteristics of this captive environment rather than fighting them is a key to helping students outside your office.

School students spend 6 to 10 hours a day in an environment that may begin at a bus stop and end at a dance, sporting event, or maybe even a homework assignment. You know where they are, and the more contacts you make with them as traditional learners; participants in athletic, academic, and social organizations; and as members of school and public communities, the greater the difference you can make. With so many things filling your day already, the secret is to use the time you already spend in the hallways, parking lots, ball games, coffee shops, and cafeterias to your best advantage.

The general factors that go into creating quality hallway contacts are the same for everyone, but the captive nature of your audience provides unique advantages. Meeting students in locations that match their changing needs becomes possible when you know where they will be and when they will be there. Observing students will tell you when they are ready to be pushed and when pushing will be counterproductive. The more time you spend in students' environments, the more you will learn, and this understanding will lead to the best choices about how, when, and where to get the most from your hallway helping skills.

Reflexes and Patience

Knowing where students are most of the day tells you much about the time pressure they are under and how much demand that puts on you to help. For example, classroom time can produce pressure for students but little demand for you to act quickly, so patience becomes a key timing factor. Once students explode into the hallways, however, it is your reflex reactions that will be tested. Keeping in mind a few classic situations allows you to make the best use of the skills you have already developed.

Hustling Reflexes

Emergency and pressured hallway situations come at the most hectic times and are often accompanied by extreme emotions. Explosions immediately after classes are commonplace as students collide physically and emotionally. Jean is most likely to be in tears near the end of a tense lunch period where major confrontations arise as everyone is trying to get in their last, best verbal shots. The heat and pressure of an after-school competition increases the chances that any statement will be taken as a personal insult demanding aggressive

words or actions. Hustling behaviors are the key to successful hallway helping at these times. Waiting for someone to come to you with
a problem is out of the question. Thinking about future plans is a
mistake. Hustling to make your actions focused, immediate, and
directed at de-escalating tensions is essential.

During these pressured times you need to remind yourself of
things you learned long ago but that can be forgotten in the rush of
the moment. The most basic reminder is to always use the lowest
possible intensity of confrontational action that will ease the situation. High-intensity actions raise the stakes for everyone and should
only be used when the stakes are already dangerously high. As a
colleague once put it for me, "You don't play an ace when a nine will
do." The reduced threat produced by low-intensity actions allows for
more flexibility in future actions. Only when low-intensity actions
prove ineffective in a given situation should you begin using higher
levels of intensity. Don't forget those directions you were given long
ago to start low and don't use your best cards unless they are clearly
needed. Table 4.1 provides a list of low- and high-intensity actions.

When one effort doesn't stop a hallway confrontation, spur-of-the-
moment alternative actions are essential. There is no time to go back
to the office to search for new techniques or consult with supervisors.
This is the time for your most ingrained skills to take over if you will
let them. Increase safety factors, acquire more support, and look for
every possible opportunity to lower tensions and stop the escalation.

Hanging Out

Students often think they need emergency help when, for the most
part, their problems call for a more casual approach. The organization of the school day, classroom seating, and regulated periods all
create a system designed to reduce emergencies. These nonemer-
gency times call for hanging out in the hallways, where your specific
goals and direct actions underlie a casual veneer.

Unlike the hustling needed during true emergencies, you can
actually give some forethought to a hanging-out approach. For example, Mary is a young 6th-grader whose mother has gone into the
hospital. Deciding to make a couple of short, physical, supportive

TABLE 4.1 Low- and High-Intensity Actions

Low Intensity Actions	High Intensity Actions
ignore	punishment
brief eye contact	glaring eye contact
subtle nonverbal movements	pointing
friendly humor	angry reactions
touching	grabbing

contacts with Mary during the day can be as easy as offering smiles, caring looks, or brief touches of encouragement on the arm. They provide Mary strength and support without having all her emotions stirred up as a direct conversation might cause.

Your planned contact with Mary only takes seconds and allows for numerous other hanging-out contacts before and after. A couple of minutes is all it takes in the hallway to congratulate Jim for an improved test score, to ask Ann whether she has taken her new medication, to point the new student in the right direction, to ask David to look out for the new student, and to show interest in the football victory with an upraised fist for Albert. Planning hanging-out efforts to provide timely support, direction, rewards, casual admonitions, and reminders to as many people as possible simply makes what you probably do naturally more consistent and effective.

Patient Presence

Emergencies and planned interactions are important opportunities, but there are many others available to you. The most chances to influence students during the day relate to more long-term objectives. Relationship building and future-oriented student objectives are the ones that require short, simple, subtle—and most important—consistent contacts over time. They call for maintaining a patient presence in students' lives.

Professionals who are seen dealing exclusively with personal traumas, testing tragedies, and scheduling screw-ups will be seen as the "shrink" or "administrator" for people with "big" problems; the kind of person you want when you are in trouble but not the person you go to for "little" worries, "normal" anxieties, or "just" thinking about the future.

Students want adults for everyday support and guidance who show genuine understanding of their lives, appreciate them, enjoy their lives as an outsider, and are easily accessible.

Taking time to maintain a patient presence in students' lives on a regular basis is really quite easy and can be done in numerous places during regular daily travels: Being visible between periods, walking through after-school practices, sitting in different places in the cafeteria, attending a dance, or mingling at a ball game. Major planning and brilliant words of wisdom are unnecessary. Consistent physical and emotional attending are the keys to developing confidence and building relationships over time.

The timing of hallway interventions will vary depending on the balance between emergency pressures and the ability to focus on long-term goals. Selecting the appropriate balance can sometimes be identified simply by observing emotional levels. One of the factors that affects those timing needs and emotional levels is the academic, personal, or social nature of the issues involved.

Environments of Change

The only legitimate reason for interventions with students is to influence the academic, personal, or social changes in their lives. Each day brings the potential to improve learning, stop a suicide, soothe a hurt, calm tensions, or head off a problem that may only be realized in the future. To be consistently effective, you need to understand three critical combinations of student environments and characteristics.

Academic Slowdown

Adults created schools for academic information gathering and skill development. This is the work of the classroom, but once out from behind classroom desks, students generally choose to deal with more personal and social issues. The result is an academic slowdown for students where studies become a much lower priority. Missing or ignoring the slowdown leads to misinterpretation of student actions and offering assistance where it is not wanted or needed. Recognizing student academic slowdown will improve your choices of which actions are most vital at a given time and where they are best employed.

Ann is a 3rd-grader whose schoolwork has fallen off drastically at about the same time her family is going through a divorce. Counseling on the family issues needs to be done in the privacy of the office, but the hallways offer an additional vehicle for growth. Brief supportive academic hallway interactions can be used to extend your helping because the content is expected and recognized as normal public information and the caring attention and sensitivity are supportive of her whole situation.

One positive aspect of student academic slow down is that although academics create great pressures in class, they can often be approached with much less tension in the hallways. A teacher immediately conveys high tension levels inside the classroom when he says, "What could you do to prepare better for the next test?" The same statement made by a counselor who regularly works the more casual hallway atmosphere carries much less anxiety-provoking baggage. The difference is that academic success or failure is the essence of classroom fears, which can raise casual statements to paramount importance.

Students know instinctively that their ownership of the hallways gives them greater permission to accept or reject your statements. Even the simple equality of having everyone in standing positions, positioned anywhere they want in the hallways, conveys more equality and power than the classroom.

The fact that students have greater freedom of choice in the hallways reduces defensiveness and increases the chances that information acquired will be used.

This is the low-pressure advantage open to counselors, coaches, club advisors, and others interacting outside the normal classroom framework that can make a major difference in a student's development.

Supplying reinforcements for success, quick statements to promote later thought, and emergency reminders of homework or tests
can all give quality visibility to the academic needs of students. They
must, however, be used in proper proportion to the personal and
social issues that generally make up the bulk of student priorities in
the hallways.

Personal Put Off

Personal issues carry considerable threat for all ages, and this is
particularly true as students approach adolescence. Resistance to
letting adults into students' personal thoughts, feelings, and worries
is a common result. The counseling office is probably the only place
that can provide the quiet, isolation, and freedom to talk openly and
honestly about such intense issues, but it can be difficult to get
students to the office when personal issues are being hidden from
adults. Hallways and gymnasiums are not places for intense personal
discussions, but they are places where you can reduce the chances
that your offers to help will be put off.

Resistance to letting adults in on personal issues is the opposite of
students' reactions to peers. It is in the hallways, bathrooms, playgrounds, streets, alleys, buses, and cars where most momentous personal decisions are discussed among peers. They select the specific
places and times to meet where adults are least likely to appear. These
are the safe places for personal openness.

*Those allowed to help with more student personal issues are the ones
who find their way to student comfort zones and lay the groundwork
there for dealing with personal issues.*

Fighting student's personal put offs in the hallways requires indirect techniques. This is no time to dive right in with, "I know you've
got personal problems that we need to discuss." A student hearing
this quickly looks around to see who might have overheard such a
stupid adult pointing out a seemingly unspeakable weakness. No
matter how true the statement is, it would be denied or ignored and
the student would leave the scene as quickly as possible.

A more productive approach for the same situation is to be attentive, supportive, relationship focused, and only vaguely suggestive. Students are more likely to deal with personal issues if they believe you recognize the situation, respect their limits, and will not press beyond their boundaries. The time you spend with students in their own environment gives you firsthand knowledge of how to best open more meaningful discussions with them. Students need to be convinced that you have seen enough of their real world to deal with them on a more equal level. This strengthening of hallway relationships is accompanied by an increased understanding of students' lives that offers additional social opportunities to make a difference.

Social Framing

Social framing is the hallway tactic with the most consistent potential for major effect. The academic context has its home in the classroom or in quiet places where books, papers, pencils, and thinking are the essential tools. Personal issues benefit most directly from intimate conversations with few people.

Because the hallways are social gathering places more than anything else, it is the social needs of students and the social framing of situations that have the greatest influence here.

Student social lives are played out in the hallways. The shy walk quickly at the sides of the hallways with their heads down. Getting to the next place to be with as little interaction as possible is the goal. The socially needy go from one person to another trying to gather as many contacts as possible without missing any new possibility that might come along. These social scavengers would never get to the next class except that the hallways eventually empty out. Most students fall in between these extremes, recognizing their need for others as well as their limited ability to consistently get those needs met. One consistency for all these social categories of students is that students develop clear patterns that can be recognized and used to construct appropriate social interventions.

Everyone knows a girl like Diane who moves from one class to the next in a consistent pattern: eyes on books, a rapid walk, staying out of heavy traffic, going directly from room to room, only looking up if absolutely necessary, and never attending extracurricular activities. Her words to you say, "Class is fine," but her hallway patterns tell you her issues are more social avoidance than academic pleasures. Once you recognize that Diane has constructed a minimal-contact social environment that eases fears at the same time it disappoints her, you can begin creating developmentally appropriate social frameworks to help.

Productive social framing should emphasize strengths and areas of confidence as new areas of weakness and doubt are gently explored. For Diane, this means the best possible construction would attach her academic knowledge and future planning to social contacts and potential relationship development. Finding Diane momentarily lingering with a group of academically oriented students would be the right framework for providing a compliment on an academic achievement. It emphasizes her strength to a group that could appreciate it. The same statement made when she was near a socially focused group could create a social setback of major proportions. Her academic prowess would be seen here as insignificant at best and insulting at worst. What could be considered support for Diane in one social framework would be a major social liability in another.

Hallway social framing is best approached more as the producer of a play than as an actor or even as a director. The task is to recognize when the right people are in the right place at the right time and then make use of the situation when it presents itself. Unlike in the office, you cannot arrange seating, introduce issues, and ensure follow-through on ideas. Instead, you rely on others for most of the interaction and continuing contact. It is the particular people you put together, where, and under what conditions that makes or breaks social framing interventions.

Expanding the Hallways

The term *hallways* has obviously been used throughout this book as a metaphor for all those casual places outside the formal office or classroom structure. Actual school hallways are the most common place to make such interventions, because everyone visits them daily, but they are certainly not the only places. As you increase your hallway interactions, you will recognize that some environments call for loud and rowdy interactions and others require soothing and soft interactions for the best communication. Deciding which to use is partly based on the environment and partly based on what is reasonable for you to accomplish.

Deafening Concert Reactions

Dealing with students at a ball game, a dance, or in the hallways often needs to be approached more like a loud concert than a school event. A parent who recently returned from a first rock concert with her child said, "My hearing may never come back, but for some reason my daughter's friends still think I'm cool. I couldn't understand the words of the songs, couldn't talk about it over the noise, and couldn't understand why people's eardrums weren't popping. Only near the end did I start enjoying myself, but I don't really know why. I was exhausted."

This parent went with her daughter expecting to listen to music, which has little to do with the attraction of a modern concert. She didn't understand because noise, commotion, and losing oneself in the event are what young people's concerts are all about; the music is secondary. Only when exhaustion caused her to give up on her own expectations and fit into what everyone else was enjoying did she become "the coolest mom" and a functional part of the event.

The helper's role in highly charged events must often be to fit in first and worry about changing students later.

Hallways, dances, and athletic contests demand loud and public reactions in order to be accepted as someone with credibility. Coaches, dance chaperons, and advisors are often sought out by students precisely because they have shown their ability to enjoy and interact within these student-chosen environments. They become a part of the event by getting into the flow, speaking louder, gesturing more obviously, and clearly enjoying what the events have to offer.

Changing the use of touch and closeness is also necessary to make yourself a viable participant under these circumstances. Much of the attraction of loud, public hallway events is that their very nature demands that personal inhibitions be lowered. As discussed previously, the loudness forces closeness and physical interaction to get messages across. Aspects of relationships must be explored here that would be seriously frowned on in most situations. Boys can hug, girls can fight, boys can cry, and girls can swear at these times with minimal stigma attached. Milling around at a sporting event, dancing in groups, and getting caught in the crush of a hallway are other low-risk rationales for making physical and social contacts that might otherwise be deemed unacceptable. When you become comfortable at interacting in these situations, you open new dimensions of potential issues to be discussed and strategies to be used.

Learning the locations where individuals and groups make themselves visible in loud ways and becoming recognized as fitting in greatly increase your credibility. Enjoying the interactions without giving up your personal and professional beliefs makes you a particularly strong role model and change agent. Effective modeling in these places requires establishing a harmony between the loudness and brashness of the situation along with the calmness and soothing qualities that you developed in traditional professional training.

Soothing Symphonies

Joining in the turmoil of a hallway location does not require giving up yourself or your beliefs to be effective. Many times it is the symphonic blending of behaviors as you stick to your most cherished beliefs that makes for the most effective helping. The "cool concert mom" was relieved to see that the drugs that appeared all around were not a part of her daughter's experience. She was thankful she didn't have to draw that line but knew that she would have if necessary to stand up for her most firmly held principles, never mind the law. She had enough hallway understanding to recognize that the kids already knew where she stood, and she would not need to set down the rules beforehand. Simply being involved and modeling demonstrated and supported her beliefs, and the trust she showed in the young people fostered better relationships. It was a blending of more obvious "cool mom" involvement, less obvious "holding back" nonactions, loud enjoyment, and quiet confidence that created a solid opportunity for adding a new positive dimension to the relationships.

There are specific actions you can use to create a limited amount of quiet and privacy in even the rowdiest situations. Consider the following actions to gain small pieces of semiprivacy in raucous environments:

- Obvious physical movements that are different from the norm of the environment get people's attention (e.g., try subtle first and go to more obvious as needed).
- Making yourself larger gets people's attention (e.g., shoulders up, sit straighter, stand taller, or, more subtly, raise your eyebrows).
- Shrinking yourself can hold attention and bring a person closer to you where communication is more effective (e.g., lower shoulders, hunch over, or lean down).
- Lowering your voice level increases attention once you have it.

Trying to change a loud, public environment into a private, quiet one just doesn't work and makes you look out of touch to boot. Effective hallway counseling with students comes about by first getting into the rhythm of the environment so that your messages will be taken as more credible. This increased hallway credibility strengthens your influence with students as they become ready to make use of your help.

Reacting to Readiness

I will never be faced with as wide a variety of readiness as I was in my first school counseling position where I handled all grade levels. Kindergartners were willing to try just about anything I asked, but their ability to think, talk, and sit still didn't fit my training at all.

The seniors, on the other hand, had plenty of ability but were unwilling to work on anything that didn't fit very precise needs and situations. It took a series of disappointing counseling efforts to teach me that the variety of school student readiness characteristics was going to be much greater than what I had faced with adults. I would need to pay close attention to what someone would be willing and able to act on effectively.

Student readiness varies with age, gender, culture, and daily events. This inconsistency can work in your favor as well as make things more difficult. Student readiness fluctuations make it possible that any minute of any day may be just the right time for helpful actions to be accepted and used by a student. The trick is to recognize high-level readiness instances and act based on the abilities and willingness presented.

Behavioral Buttressing

The skills and knowledge that make up ability are what are taught most directly and most often in schools. Hallways, lunch rooms, playgrounds, gyms, and streets are the worst places to introduce knowledge and abilities, but these are great places to clarify and fortify learning in real-life situations. Behavioral buttressing of the abilities that have been taught elsewhere is the best use of hallway helping to improve the ability aspect of readiness.

Gwenn had no idea how to start explaining her situation to others when she first came to see her counselor. In the privacy of the office, the counselor gave her a book and then discussed with her the specific information and actions she needed to consider. The counselor reminded her of health class lectures and handouts even as she scoffed at the idea that these could have any practical value. The hallways would have been the absolute worst place to supply such information or to have Gwenn study and process it. On the other hand, they are exactly the right place for Gwenn to practice what she learned. It is in the hallways where Gwenn will speak to others of her pregnancy, be assertive of her needs, and respond to looks and comments.

Practice in the hallways provides the opportunity for you to evaluate skill development and set up reinforcements for productive new behaviors along with disincentives for behaviors that don't work.

Leave the responsibility of introducing concepts, skills, and abilities to the classroom teacher, the office session, the tutor, and the parent. Sticking to the functional strengths of hallways to buttress the learning of abilities will increase your hallway helping potential and decrease the chances of your making serious mistakes. Limiting what you try to accomplish will also leave you more time to attend to a student's willingness, which is taught less directly or effectively in schools.

Wary Willingness

Teaching students what, why, and how to act is a far cry from getting them to take appropriate actions. Many of us forget this from time to time as we try to teach students life skills they already know but simply choose not to practice. The reason for their lack of action is generally not some missing piece of ability but instead a lack of willingness to match the risks of potential action.

Hallway helpers watch for student willingness to risk in different situations, respect willingness levels, and improve the support systems that can appropriately increase one's willingness to act.

Student willingness has to do with matching changing comfort and confidence levels with risk levels that escalate or de-escalate as situations evolve. Hallway interventions that match student discomfort and lowered confidence with high-risk situations are bound to fail. Reading willingness levels wrong can lead to pushing a student into a situation in which embarrassment will be the primary outcome. Reading willingness correctly can put a student in a situation in which he or she can find success in overcoming a meaningful obstacle.

Consider a boy you would like to influence who has recently become a member of a local gang. He might reject attention during a tense gang situation but be more willing to communicate with you in a less risky environment. When high anxiety best defines some-one's willingness level, offering support through reinforcements or encouraging safe actions are the only viable techniques.

There are also those times when rejection of your efforts or anxiety over consequences is not what is driving a student's willingness to act. These are the times when students are confident that they can speak or act effectively in a given situation. Your role in the case of confident students encompasses several basic hallway tasks.

Let them act as they will. Encourage confident students to act on their own beliefs and ideas. The only times to reconsider this are when you are specifically invited to offer direction or when you are afraid the natural consequences of a student's actions are both seri-ous and irreparable.

Point out potential actions sparingly. Nothing squashes a student's confidence like overdirecting them. Successfully carrying out your good ideas will provide nowhere near the potential growth as actions they choose by themselves.

Arrange for appropriate reinforcements to be in place. Students need to be reinforced most for their positive personal and social actions. Spend your time putting mechanisms in place to reward productive hallway behaviors. These might include bringing together people who will naturally be appreciative of positive actions, getting your-self in the right place to be able to compliment on a positive action, and creating a schoolwide reward system that supports positive actions in the hallways. Every high school has an athletic trophy case, so why not create another for "Hallway Heroes" that calls attention to the social and personal accomplishments of students and graduates.

Help evaluate the natural consequences. Confident students will act on their own no matter what you say. Your efforts should attend to the aftermath of actions and helping people evaluate the conse-quences of their words and behaviors.

Be ready to pick up the pieces. One of the dangers of confidence is that ability can be misjudged based on poor comparisons to past successes. Your analysis of what people are trying to do and their ability to do it puts you in a position to catch those who have had a failure. Remember also that failure is a learning tool, and it is not your role to prevent failure.

You can serve students by getting them back on their feet when they have been knocked down and helping them to learn from their mistakes.

The seemingly unlimited and constantly changing characteristics of individual students make work with them seem exciting, rewarding, complex, and sometimes nearly impossible. Using hallway techniques is a way to expand the opportunities for seeing and interacting with students in their most natural environment. The more comfortable you become with that environment outside your office, the more consistencies you will see in their world. This more accurate picture of student needs and behavior patterns will allow you to make consistent and more effective developmental use of multiple, brief hallway encounters with students.

The increased opportunities to help students that hallway encounters provide can be multiplied even further by including adults in the hallway helping model. This is no easy task, because not all other adults will have your abilities and motivation. The next chapter offers ideas on how to use hallway strategies to help encourage adults to become more effective at developing their own hallway potential.

5

Activating Adult Motivators

Making a realistic commitment to provide the best possible service to young people carries the obligation to involve others who are part of the school environment. Getting these adults on our side seemed like a straightforward task when we were newly indoctrinated professionals. Books and instructors explained how the roles of counselors, teachers, administrators, mental health professionals, parents, secretaries, service employees, and community members were all designed to form an efficient working team. A few days on the job made it clear that such a "team" is not easily created, strengthened, or maintained—no matter what the books said. Getting the most effective teamwork from professional and nonprofessional adults requires more personal persuasion than rules, regulations, or theory. It requires personal time and attention to the human being inside the formal role. Even the best of us can forget or ignore the personal needs and limitations of adults.

We sometimes act with adults in ways we would consider uncaring, unprofessional, or even unethical if we did the same with students.

A wonderful counselor from Oregon taught me this important lesson at a national convention several years ago. We met at a crowded reception and quickly found a common bond in our work to improve school climate and our frustrations over not making all the progress we sought. Vicki was bringing the joy, enthusiasm, and stories she found in music to improve the environment of whole schools. I have no musical talent at all, but I loved what she was doing and we eagerly searched for ideas on how to improve on her successes.

Vicki's only major frustration with her work was that she couldn't reach the level of involvement from professionals and other adults related to the school that she got willingly from students. We knew that greater adult commitment was critical if the enthusiasm and actions her programs generated were to continue after she left. So we whined together for a few minutes about how responsible professionals and parents are "supposed to act." Tears welling up in Vicki's eyes made it clear she had recognized something else that was missing:

I'm just realizing that I don't treat adults in the school with the same care, attention, and forgiveness that I treat the students. I attend to students as real people with human needs and fallibilities while I treat the professionals and parents more like robots that are required to do their jobs as expected. Why should they be personally excited like the students? Why should they trust in me and my ideas? Why should they think this will be good for them as well as students? I don't follow through on my most important beliefs with adults the same way I do with students. That's what's wrong!

One side effect of Vicki's tears was a simple confirmation of my status as anything but the life of a party. More important, however, was the realization that we needed to be more attentive to the human side of adults in order to tap their maximum potential for helping children. We recalled how our most effective professional relationships were those where personal understanding, trust, caring, and support were obviously present. The less these were a part of the relationship, the narrower was the scope of how we were able to help. Vicki and I left the party excited that we had a new direction for being more effective in schools: We vowed that we would be more attentive to the human being inside the adult.

It's easy to get overwhelmed with the seemingly unlimited complications surrounding the personal, professional, societal, and situational characteristics of relationships. The more we learn, the more complex they become. We know relationships will be significantly affected by gender, age, race, culture, developmental stage, family functioning, economics, intelligence, creativity, and a myriad of other factors. It's enough to make you want to throw up your hands and say, "I quit! I can't handle any more!"

No professional can take every personal and situational characteristic into account all the time. We just don't have that much mental and emotional capacity. Successful professionals categorize this knowledge in their minds so they can quickly identify a few motivators that will most likely get desired results with a given person or situation.

Three general motivators of adults in school situations that need continual care and attention from the effective hallway helper are power, vulnerability, and joy.

You can feel confident that no matter what other issues are involved, these will play a major part in determining how to get the most productive school involvement out of any adult.

Power

Power is a word that becomes overly formalized in schools where it is clearly attached to positions, ranks, or other titles. We tend to presume that the people who hold formal titles and positions have power and the will to use it, whereas others without rank lack power altogether. As schools have become more and more based on structured tasks and roles and less on personal relationships, a greater emphasis has been given to this formal power. Such a situation might have some validity if formal power actually worked as well as planned, but it never does.

The informal power of a persistent student, loud parent, willing teacher, reliable bus driver, or trusted counselor is often much more influential than any formal position. However, the fearful teacher, defensive administrator, embarrassed parent, or hesitant counselor will give up potential power and influence because of their misconceptions or anxieties. You can vastly increase your hallway influence by being regularly attentive to three aspects of power:

- The commonly exaggerated and often inappropriate attention given to formal positions of power
- The massive amount of informal power that goes unrecognized
- The effects of people's power misperceptions

Hallway relationship building gives recognition to formal powers that serve to maintain stability within the school. Creating and adapting to change, however, are best supported by strengthening the informal power available to all individuals and groups. One person with formal power can "tell someone to act," but it is the much greater numbers of people with informal power available to them that will determine whether, when, where, and how appropriate actions will be.

- The more people you move from the position of uninvolved bystanders to people who recognize and act on their informal power potential, the healthier a community becomes through greater sharing of power and responsibility.
- The effective use of informal hallway power incorporates a variety of "soft" strategies. These soft approaches downplay demanding forms of power that often lead to resentment and defeat in hallway interactions. Your formal power interventions are

best saved for critical times in private sessions where egos will not be so challenged. Some samples of an almost infinite number of soft hallway strategies with adults include the following:

Building cooperative approaches rather than individual initiatives

Maintaining a relaxed, confident posture in tense, difficult situations

Listening and reflecting much more than telling and directing

Encouraging mild hallway confrontations on issues, but avoiding hallway confrontations on personalities

Using mediation for win–win situations rather than conflict for who-wins

Showing respect even when you don't feel it's deserved

Never commenting on private information in public

Encouraging only actions that can be accomplished in public

De-escalating tensions rather than giving in to frustrations

Schools that achieve the most positive changes in academics, discipline, and climate invariably report how all groups of adults and students feel more involved, encouraged, and empowered. It is an empowerment that authority cannot delegate but instead must be identified and implemented through personal insights and supportive relationships. These are the supportive relationships and soft-power strategies you can use in normal daily interactions to promote adult strengths and helps adults to overcome misconceptions and self-doubt that stand in the way of them giving their best possible efforts.

Vulnerability

The degree to which people feel vulnerable to harm will influence how much risk they take and how much effort they give in a particular situation. Encouraging people rather than demanding change requires attention to the origins of an individual's tension and anxieties. An essential step to hallway success is recognizing the different causes of adult feelings of vulnerability related to schools. Only with these understandings in hand can hallway strategies be selected with the confidence they will lower or sometimes raise an adult's levels of vulnerability to make them as effective as possible.

Our actions toward others frequently ignore how vulnerable many adults actually feel in school situations.

Students may get report cards, but it is adults who are under the most pressure when the question of what went wrong comes up.

Adults are the ones who receive the eventual blame and feel the guilt for a lack of student learning, violence, inadequate school conditions, a lack of resources, or a poor home environment. Just thinking about the potential failure of the youth in our care is enough to tie knots in our stomachs.

Adults handle their vulnerability in a multitude of more and less effective ways, including tears, concern, determination, anger, blaming, talking, screaming, and silence. They may strike out, politely ask for attention, isolate themselves, or switch reactions at times and places so that their actions seem to make no sense at all. Although some of these reactions are more socially acceptable ways of demonstrating "vulnerability" than others, they all represent a common concern for the survival of an adult's professional and personal self-worth.

Your effectiveness increases as you give more attention to those things that make an adult feel vulnerable, recognize what conditions trigger the reactions, and act to mediate the vulnerability. Someone's vulnerability is rarely brought up in conversation. More often, it is attended to by adapting interactions to take the threats into account. Only when an adult's vulnerabilities are held in proper perspective can people make the most of their abilities and find the excitement and pleasure that exist all around in school interactions.

Joy

A major force that drives adults to work positively in schools is the joy of personal involvement in the lives of young people and other adults. If consideration of individual power and vulnerability seem like minefields to traverse, joy is an area that you can approach from a more straightforward direction. Adults want good things for children in schools, and they will be most happy and useful when you help them find active, creative, effective, and personally satisfying ways to be involved.

A simple smile is recognized by aware adults as the unspoken message, "Thank you so very much." They understand when a parent's sigh of relief means, "Bless you for helping." And they are the adults who gain joy from the little ways in which appreciation is shown for their efforts. Those who work the best and the hardest for schools are the ones who realize the joy in their efforts, and the more people can be helped to recognize that joy, the better for everyone.

Using techniques that tap an adult's sense of joy at being involved with children and the school greatly increases your overall influence on the total school environment as well as on those specific individuals and their children. Joy-tapping asks little more than calling attention to pleasures and successes already present but perhaps not recognized.

It is easy to overlook the everyday joy of doing good things as we are fully involved with people. Adults in particular are presumed to "know" that they are in the middle of enjoyable and worthy circumstances, but that is a false presumption.

We all need continual reminders to examine and cherish our personal sources of joy and accomplishments.

Hallway helping takes every opportunity to encourage these positive, reflective looks. The external rewards for joy-recognizing actions are an invigorated atmosphere and more motivated adults seeking ways of being productively involved in the school.

The influence that comes with official positions is an important component of maintaining social stability and physical safety. But the nature of official roles and formal responsibilities, as well as the physical structure of buildings, offices, and classrooms, can also cause a system to underuse individual motivation, knowledge, skills, creativity, and outside input. Brief, casual, personally empowering, threat-lowering, and joy-illuminating hallway strategies serve to strengthen the system by reinvigorating adults who come in contact with it.

These three school-related motivators apply to all adults, but not in equal amounts nor in the same ways to everyone. Teachers, administrators, staff, parents, and others are influenced differently based on their unique situations. These differences must be taken into account in order to increase the respect and influence all adults feel, thereby creating a better balance with formal power gained from the system.

Tailoring Strategies for Teachers

Teachers have far more contact with students than anyone else during the school day, giving them enormous potential for influence. Tapping that influence potential requires strategies that encourage teachers to take a more accurate, positive, growth-oriented, and enjoyable approach to their workday. Specific techniques are selected based on an understanding of the power and vulnerability of teachers and taking appropriate actions to reflect them.

Balance Power and Vulnerability

A major factor in teachers' motivation is the extreme contrast in their power and vulnerability depending on whether they are inside or outside the classroom. Inside the classroom they have virtually total official power over where students sit, what they do, when they talk, and what they discuss.

Outside the classroom unofficial influence reigns as students pay more attention to those people they value and respect as persons and less to formal positions of power.

This influence transition makes teachers much more vulnerable outside the classroom than inside. Many never become comfortable with the continuous shifting of necessary perspectives and skills. In order to protect themselves and bring consistency to their lives, they often settle for either ruling the classroom with an iron fist or being a buddy in the hallways. Making either direction their model creates an influence vacuum, greater vulnerability, and less enjoyment in the other location.

Your hallway skills and knowledge can help teachers become more comfortable at shifting their approach to students and parents from "classroom boss" to "respected individual" and back again as the situation calls for it. This hallway assistance can be offered and reinforced within real-life situations rather than in counseling or training sessions. For example, you can

- Make sure to support the teacher as an equal or better in every situation, thereby confirming his or her power and reducing feelings of vulnerability

- Give recognition to the different situations, feelings, and behaviors involved when conflicts occur between classroom and hallway pressures

- Call attention to the different ways some adults gain influence in one setting and give it away in others. Ask reflective questions on why that might be so and how one could change for the better

- Note the differences in whom students pay attention to outside the classroom and explore what could be done to gain such influence

Showcase Success

Teachers know what makes them feel good at school; they just don't take time to pay much attention to it. It is knowing that the look of excitement and satisfaction in someone's face is a result of their efforts that can make teachers feel appreciated. It is there to be seen when someone does well on a test, makes the volleyball team, finds a new friend, sees her child win an award, or finally understands an idea that he never thought he would get. Unfortunately, teachers get tired and frustrated, and are often too busy, too tied up in thoughts, or too burned out to see these signs of their own success.

Teachers often miss the best parts of being teachers: the parts that go furthest toward making them caring, motivated, and student oriented.

A particularly pleasant hallway strategy is highlighting the joy of teacher successes when they may be going unrecognized. The task only takes looking for the positive outcomes that teachers cause and pointing them out to the teacher, as the following examples show.

- "John is awfully proud. You must be pleased."
- "I bet Ms. Thompson never expected such a friendly welcome. She really left pleased, didn't she?"
- "Can I sit in on one of your classes sometime? I hear kids talking about working their butts off there, and I'd love to see it."
- "The principal seems relaxed; you must have gotten things to run smoothly."

These samples are not the simple positive reinforcement they might appear to be at first glance. You are not really giving reinforcement at all but instead calling attention to reinforcements that are naturally present. The better you come to know the school, teachers, and students, the more obvious the reinforcements become. Using them to help teachers see the everyday joy they create provides the positive outlook that will be good for everyone.

Multiply Low-Impact Contacts

There are plenty of opportunities to work with teachers in casual settings before, during, and after school, so there is no need to get everything done at once. Using conservative small steps is the hallway helping rule as you work primarily for progress over time through multiple low-impact contacts. Time-limited, difficult decisions are best left to private places where concentration is easier and more time can be taken to make quality plans.

Professional issues have a particularly good fit with the multiple low-impact contacts model. Everyone has unspoken expectations that teachers will be professionals virtually all the time and certainly when they are in a school setting. Reacting to teachers in this context conveys permission to talk about professional issues without draw-ing the undue attention that an overheard personal or social discus-sion might attract. You can use this professional context to take an indirect approach to any number of other issues. Consider just one personal and one social context example to get your thinking started:

- A teacher depressed over marital problems will not be cured but could still benefit from positive support given about a student's success or the excitement of his students about class.
- An inappropriately self-isolated teacher could be socially en-couraged by your seeking of information through a casual discussion of a school issue that included several teachers.

The low-impact aspect of these interactions has long-range value because of the numerous opportunities available, and it is essential because of situational and time pressures. Teachers in the hallways have a tremendous amount going on around them. They must simul-taneously evaluate what just happened in class or elsewhere; act on what is happening right now; and prepare for what they will have to do shortly. They cannot deal effectively with major issues in the hallways without ignoring more immediate concerns. Numerous low-impact interactions fit these timing needs best when they focus attention on what is happening, what just happened, or what is about to happen. The closer your interactions are to the immediate time press of the teacher, the greater impact they are likely to have.

As the importance of issues rises, you must increasingly seek more private places and additional quiet time. The office certainly fits these criteria, but it may also provide more formality than would be best. Middle-ground places that fall between hectic hallway environments and formal offices are places like the cafeteria when it is not lunch-time, the local coffee shop, the teacher's lounge, the local library, or just a short walk during a planning period, before school, or at day's end. This small sample of middle-ground locations offers a positive reason to be there, more privacy than the hallways, a slower pace, and the opportunity to take a break from the immediate teacher responsibilities. Selecting the right amount of formality, casualness, privacy, and necessary time is decided based on your evaluation of need and readiness of the teacher to be helped.

Hear the Unsaid "No"

Teachers have students, parents, administrators, and state regulators continuously pushing them to do more with less. That they become self-protective and hesitant about accepting anything new or different should be no surprise. In a way, it is amazing that teachers continue to seek improvement on professional, personal, and social fronts as often as they do. You can support this growth motivation with strategies that attend to the teacher struggles that influence their willingness and ability to think new thoughts, experience new feelings, and try new behaviors.

Most teachers experience a relaxed pleasure in the school environment when they are successful students, but once they become teachers that environment takes a more threatening turn. The successful student learned how to enjoy taking in information and giving it back as required by an authority figure. The switch to being the authoritative information source and controller of the process is not an easy one. This new role contains greater pressure to meet more people's expectations than any student experiences they may have had. How willing a teacher is to recognize and act on your hallway interactions will be directly related to how well you attend to his signs of unwillingness.

It would be nice if professionals who were unwilling to do something would just tell you "No," but it usually isn't that simple. Pride and determination to meet other peoples' expectations often push us to look for indirect ways to avoid something rather than to take the direct approach. Consider some common signs we have all recognized that appear when helpful initiatives are greeted with an unsaid "No":

- Looking elsewhere while feigning attention to you (I can't give you my full attention and therefore cannot be held to my answer.)
- Suddenly nervous movements of head, eyes, feet, or hands (This contact is making me anxious, and I might lie to get away.)

- A quick acknowledgment of your contact followed by immediately exiting the situation (I had to leave too quickly to be responsible for my answer.)
- Looking around for someone else as if really needing to see that person (I could not attend to you because there was a more important need.)
- Avoiding eye contact as you approach (I cannot run away, so I'll pretend I don't see you.)
- "Sure, just talk to me again about it" (No way will I consider that, but I'll get you off my back, and maybe you'll forget.)

It is important to tread carefully on the willingness of teachers, because they have so much invested in looking professional and not making mistakes.

Too much pressure often results in teachers actively avoiding your input and even subverting your work with others.

Always leave room to lower the intensity of relationships based on your recognition of discomfort and unwillingness on the part of a teacher.

Involving the Principal

The individual most often responsible for setting the overall tone of a school is the building principal, so influencing that person's efforts can have major significance. Holding the highest formal position brings the principal maximum credit for a school's successes and also the most blame for its failures. This combination of formal power and high vulnerability is a potent mixture that drives principals in one of two directions. Those who focus on gaining credit and success become highly visible and aggressively push for productive changes. Others seeking security from their vulnerability shy away from the dangers of visibility and stifle change. Leaving the principal out of your intentional hallway interactions discounts a major influence on school climate. On the other hand, giving direct attention to casual interactions with administrators can go far toward invigorating a school's atmosphere.

Hallway efforts to influence principals focus on perceptions of a principal's power rather than official job duties.

When staff, students, parents, and principals themselves have faith in the position and the person, tremendous power becomes available for positive use. You can help create a healthier school climate by spending some energy caring for this fragile power and feeding ideas and information that bring out a principal's best for those you care for most.

Reach Out First and Often

If you want schools to move in directions you desire and principals to make decisions you think are best, then take the initiative rather than "hoping" for things to go your way. Regularly make the first move to get your agenda on the table and keep it there.

Feed Organizational Needs

The way to a principal's heart is through improving the orderly flow of ideas and actions. Give confirmation when things are working right; publicly support productive changes; help clarify the realities of problem situations; and offer alternative procedures for problem areas. Many of you will question whether your principal will listen to any of this—and you may be right to wonder. But although they may not give you credit for it, the fact remains that administrators get most of their ideas from others whom they trust—and one of those others might as well be you.

Personalize Relationships

The most effective principals have personalized relationships with a wide variety of students, parents, community leaders, and teachers. Occasionally reminding them of names, people to commend, upcoming community events, or the special times in a student's, teacher's, or parent's life encourages more personalized contact with more students and adults. The more of these contacts they have, the more likely they are to respond to the human needs of the school.

Maintain Touch With the Real World

It is remarkably easy for principals to become isolated in their offices. One principal put it this way: "Problems, headaches, and more problems; all this without taking a step out of the office. I'm a damn captive, and when the problems are gone, I'm afraid to step outside and see what's coming next."

Effective principals are visibly active in the hallways, classrooms, playgrounds, and community. The more of that you can promote, the better it is for the school. Inviting a principal into a classroom guidance session, dragging one out of the office to enjoy the hallways, or generally calling attention to these times and places where they can see what the rest of the real world is doing are all pluses for increased understanding and realistic decision making.

Appreciating Specialists

Teacher and principal positions are given a much wider range of official powers than the remainder of the staff. Counselors, psychologists, social workers, secretaries, custodians, cooks, and bus drivers have much less authority to direct student thoughts and actions. The result is that staff must make many more questionable judgment calls on how to best fulfill their roles. What value is placed on their ideas or actions? How should they raise difficult issues? Whose toes will be stepped on? How much effort should they make in situations that don't directly affect their responsibilities? When do they get involved, and when should they keep their noses out of a bad scene? This vagueness about the breadth of specialists' roles in promoting the overall school climate is the key factor to consider when approaching hallway interactions with them.

Although most schools have specialists who do their limited jobs well, the best schools have staff who are involved in school affairs well beyond the confines of formal job descriptions. The custodian who attends school board meetings, the psychologist who keeps score at basketball games, the secretary who attends faculty meetings, and the bus driver who is an assistant football coach each add to a more unified school community. These actions break down role barriers and encourage a more holistic approach to maintaining a healthy school. And it is just these types of actions that hallway strategies can encourage and support by validating contributions, reinforcing professional responsibilities, and promoting expanded involvement efforts.

Validate Specialties

Respect is the foundation for any positive relationship, and it can be first communicated to school specialists through validations of their position, work, and related accomplishments. People in these positions do not get the automatic recognition when a school succeeds that comes to teachers and principals. Unless they are provided specific reinforcements to validate themselves, problematic feelings of disinterest, discouragement, and resentment are likely to become the norm.

> *Hallway strategies with staff begin with communicating casual and consistent appreciative recognition of the value and quality of each specialist's work.*

Promoting staff member efforts that go beyond specific work assignments can only be accomplished when cooks, secretaries, psychologists, and counselors first feel valued for the work they are specifically hired to do.

Attend to the Little Extras

Hallway strategies that influence the most people give attention to those ideas and actions that go only "slightly beyond" basic professional obligations. This form of social–behavioral shaping fits the nature of specialists' positions that do not encourage them to step outside specifically assigned tasks. Cooks cannot be required to advise students, counselors wouldn't be told to help keep the buses

running, and secretaries aren't asked to teach English skills. Reinforcing broader school involvement on the part of competent but uninvolved staff members requires regular attention to the smallest of
steps. The bus driver who comments on a student needs to be
thanked immediately and reminded of the value of the comment at
a later time. The cook who one day adds a few hand-picked flowers
to the lunch counter needs to be specifically complimented. The
psychologist who leaves a handwritten note with an assessment
needs encouragement for taking the extra time to personalize. Remembering to give recognition and support when staff members do
the little extras is no new technique, but it is an easy one to forget in
the rush of the day.

Support Public Risking

The further staff members go beyond specified responsibilities,
the greater are the risks they take. Public support is needed to
encourage such actions, because even the most innocent movements
away from designated roles make well-meaning people anxious and
threatened. Someone will question the audacity of the secretary who
first volunteers to teach staff and students what she learned at a
recent workshop. A custodian and social worker who come together
to a monthly board of education meeting will be bombarded with
mildly stated and harsher unstated questions about their possible
motivation for such an unheard of act. When the assistant coach of
the volleyball team is also a cook, many will wonder, what is the story
here?

> *Publicly, physically, verbally, and socially showing appreciation for
> people who step into uncharted waters is central to hallway helping
> of staff. These are the ways you demonstrate the belief that individual
> human beings have greater value to the school community than any
> job description can ever specify.*

Hallway strategies emphasize the value of people's specific roles,
attend to personal factors, and promote risk-taking actions that make
greater use of their talents. This expansion of school staff involve-

ment also increases the ability to tap parent and community resources.

Forging Parental Partnerships

A frail mother with three small children standing just ahead of me at the supermarket handed the cashier some food stamps for groceries and just enough cash to pay for one small book. The little book promised easy steps to making better students out of the hellions running around her. I doubted if anything could make a difference, but I also wondered what treat or even necessity this woman was passing up for the hope of providing a better education for her children? What other things did she forego to improve their learning? One quick look at bookstore shelves demonstrates that this woman may have been poorer than most but similar in motivation. The enormous number of books on parenting and parental relationships with schools is convincing evidence that information and adult resources available outside the school walls is tremendous. What is needed is a forging of cooperative partnerships that invite and invest this wealth of adult resources into our efforts with young people.

The most successful schools are the ones that have formed solid relationships with parents and communities. A mutual involvement by these groups builds understanding, trust, and commitment to each other by breaking down the barriers of brick walls, formal power structures, and social snobbery. Hallway helping techniques are partnership-building tools that reach beyond formal offices, structured classrooms, and official positions to meet people on common ground and more equal footing. They are the casual means by which parent–school tensions can be reduced and the natural joys of learning recognized.

Power and vulnerability are the most important sources of tension when outsiders come into contact with school personnel.

Parents are likely to sense that they will be looked down on because of the school personnel's training and formal roles with students. Whether or not professionals feel or communicate these ideas, the perceived power differential raises the stakes for outsiders and makes them highly vulnerable. Any interactions with the goal of forging more equal partnerships must decrease this perceived power differential in order to realize the positive benefits.

The joy of seeing children learn and knowing you play a part is the strongest positive motivator for adult involvement in education. This is a common bonding element for school–community partnerships that hallway strategies can regularly bring into everyone's consciousness. Hallway helping uses multiple ways to point up the pleasures of helping children learn, whether it's preparing them for a test, reading together, arguing over new ideas, or finding the best bargain at the supermarket. These are not complex strategies; they require little academic study; and they don't take great concentration. What they do demand to maintain their value is frequent use with as many adults as possible.

Locate Relaxed Adults

Relaxed occasions and locations are the times and places to make yourself a real person in the eyes of nonschool adults. These are little league games, street corners, church bazaars, blacktop basketball courts, carnivals, and fishing holes.

Find out where the adults you want to affect go to relax, take yourself there, and bump into them not so accidentally.

Watch, relax, be involved, and get a sense of what your potential partners are like in their comfort zone. The strongest partnerships are the ones that share relaxed time as well as business time.

Meet Where Adults Are Confident

Equalize power differentials between yourself and outsiders by meeting where they are most confident. Meeting parents in the office, classroom, or somewhere else in the school is great for professionals, but these are also places where a parent's confidence is lowest. When a parent is asked to meet at school, chances are 90% that something is wrong and they will arrive prepared for the worst. Casual meetings at parents' homes, offices, a mall, or a coffee shop can be used as alternative meeting places to reduce tension, increase parent confidence, and promote the sharing of responsibilities.

Find Something to Support

Building relationships with a wide variety of adults requires giving support to the most obnoxious adults as well as the most pleasant. This is no easy task, but it is an important one.

Long-term outcomes are best when you highlight something valuable about the individual in every relationship interaction.

I once had a parent come up to me in a parking lot, furious about his daughter seeing me for counseling. I was intolerant of the fact that he abused his daughter and wife, angry at his accusatory and threatening behavior toward me, and I resented his ruining my weekend. I didn't hide my feelings, but it took all the parking lot patience I could muster to also express my appreciation for his coming directly to me and then to explain how, when, and where he could file charges against me. I figured I'd give him the rope to hang himself by encouraging him to bring things out into the open. As I expected, no charges were filed, but surprisingly, he later asked me to help him find a counselor. He told me that no one had ever tried to help him when he was that angry, and when he calmed down, he realized I was someone who could be trusted.

Give a Psychological Massage

Let business issues, answers, and problems occasionally go by the wayside when someone needs special stroking. It is easier to justify this in casual relationship building than in the office or classroom, where work, goals, and time on task generally take priority. Give everyone a break once in a while and just make a couple of people feel better about themselves. The effort can pay partnership dividends later as people realize something of your caring for them even when you wind up on different sides of an issue.

Regardless of the results on the issue, the sense of caring promotes continuation of the partnership and potential for progress.

Repeat Yourself

Anything that can be done once in the hallways is better done repeatedly. One brief supportive gesture, friendly word, statement of praise, or expression of comfort may have little value in itself. Repetition and consistency make the long-term difference.

Human nature dims the joy of one interaction quickly and causes doubt about its real meaning. This is particularly true for adults who have years of negative learning experiences that must be unlearned. Only when you consistently meet, greet, and attend to people with positive casual interactions do you cement understanding of the major benefits in a solid partnership.

Make Preemptive Contacts

Private interactions often deal with problems that have arisen, whereas hallway strategies emphasize relationship building before a crisis. It only takes a little experience to recognize what crises are likely to occur, when to expect them, and which parents will probably be involved. This information should help you head off negative crises, soften the impact of others, and even promote crises that have positive potential. Hallway strategies are much more effective when they are used over time in developmental ways.

Meet Outside More Than Inside

This is a simple numbers issue. Making more brief hallway contacts with parents off the school grounds than within the building lowers tension levels, improves trust, creates a more equal responsibility for partnerships, and produces stronger relationships over time. Once you recognize that you are having regular contacts with a parent in school, it should signify that your roles are likely becoming rigid and one-sided and call for spending more time in the parent's world. Positive telephone calls and individual notes count for these contacts, as well as shopping mall hellos, ball games, and home visits.

Get Down

This is a basic concept that is so easy to forget. To downplay your potential threat and increase the confidence of a parent, always sit, stand, or kneel lower than them. Take the smaller chair, stand on the next lower step, lean on something to shrink your height, or kneel if you must, but don't ever stand when a parent is sitting. This is essential body language and goes a long way in convincing someone that ideas and actions are more important to you than official positions.

Building more equal parent partnerships requires you to make the extra gestures of openness, respect, and equality in order to show that your part in the relationship comes more from who you are than what position you hold or what extra education you have. They will increase your influence on the entire school community and, in turn, bring you some of the personal and professional benefits we all desire.

Reminders

Once you have the training and experience needed to be an effective professional, helping in the hallways becomes a matter of using your skills consistently and reflexively in those places where your training didn't guide you. Plying your skills outside the office and classroom will not be in the job description, but doing so carries benefits beyond those available in your traditional work environment. I would like to end with a few key reminders of basic concepts that should help keep you focused on what you are doing as hallway helpers and why you are doing it.

1. The more positive and therapeutic brief contacts you make with people related to the school, the more you can change uninvolved bystanders into helpful contributors. The most productive and supportive school environments for everyone, including yourself, are those that are continuously involving more and more people as contributors to the health of the school community.

2. Most of your day is spent outside your office already. Hallway helping is simply a better way of using that time and those places.

3. Schedules and rules of schools tell you where people are and what they will be doing. This organization allows you to plan for even the most casual of encounters throughout the day.

4. The multiple and unending nature of potential hallway helping opportunities allows for the use of goals and actions that are limited in duration and scope, developmental in nature, and flexible enough to change over time. You don't have to get it all done at once.

5. There are more than enough low-impact hallway opportunities available to allow for innovative strategies and making up for mistakes you might make. Final outcomes are not riding on each interaction, so relax a little and enjoy your hallway possibilities.

References and Suggested Readings

Blanchard, K., & Johnson, S. (1982). *The one-minute manager.* New York: William Morrow.

Gottfredson, G. D., & Gottfredson, D. C. (1985). *Victimization in schools.* New York: Plenum Press.

Hazler, R. J. (1996). *Breaking the cycle of violence: Interventions for bullying and victimization.* Washington, DC: Accelerated Development.

Kottler, J. A. (1997). *Succeeding with difficult students.* Thousand Oaks, CA: Corwin Press.

McGuffin, P. W. (1991). The effect of timeout duration on frequency of aggression in hospitalized children with conduct disorders. *Behavioral Residential Treatment, 6,* 279–299.

Miller, G. E., & Prinz, R. J. (1990). Enhancement of social learning family interventions for childhood conduct disorders. *Psychological Bulletin, 108*(2), 291–307.

National Education Goals Panel. (1993). *The national education goals report—Volume 1: The national report.* Washington, DC: U.S. Government Printing Office.

Office of Prisons Annual Report. (1996). Columbus: State of Ohio Printing Office.

Sklare, G. B. (1997). *Brief counseling that works: A solution-focused approach for school counselors.* Thousand Oaks, CA: Corwin Press.

Statistical Abstract of the United States. (1995). Washington, DC: U.S. Government Printing Office.

Talmon, M. (1990). *Single session therapy.* San Francisco: Jossey-Bass.

Toch, T. (1993). Violence in the schools. *U.S. News & World Report.* November 8, 31–47.

CORWIN
PRESS

The Corwin Press logo—a raven striding across an open book—represents the happy union of courage and learning. We are a professional-level publisher of books and journals for K–12 educators, and we are committed to creating and providing resources that embody these qualities. Corwin's motto is "Success for All Learners."